A Gift for

_____

From

_____

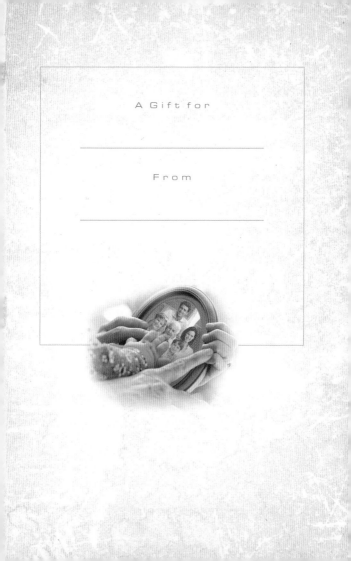

"The most important thing I have done for my grandchildren is to pray for them. Even when I may not know where they are or their specific needs, I pray to my all-knowing Father in heaven and then He reaches down to them and works in their lives according to His perfect will.

The greatest legacy you can leave to your grandchildren is your prayers for them, for God will keep on answering them, even after you are in heaven, until He has accomplished His purposes for those prayers. Here is a marvelous book that will inspire and teach you new things about your awesome privilege of enlisting the help of the God of the universe into the lives of your grandchildren."

EVELYN CHRISTENSON
AUTHOR, *What Happens When Women Pray*

A GRANDMOTHER'S GUIDE

— T O —

Praying

FOR HER FAMILY

Nancy Ann Yaeger

BETHANY HOUSE PUBLISHERS
Minneapolis, Minnesota

A Grandmother's Guide to Praying for Her Family
Copyright © 2006, Nancy Ann Yaeger

Cover and interior design: The DesignWorks Group; cover, David Uttley; interior, Robin Black. www.thedesignworksgroup.com

Published by Bethany House Publishers
11400 Hampshire Avenue South
Bloomington, Minnesota 55438

Bethany House Publishers is a division of Baker Publishing Group, Grand Rapids, Michigan.

Printed in China

ISBN-13: 978-0-7642-0190-5
ISBN-10: 0-7642-0190-5

Library of Congress Cataloging-in-Publication Data

Yaeger, Nancy Ann.
   A grandmother's guide to praying for her family / Nancy Ann Yaeger.
      p. cm.
   Summary: "This year-round prayer guide gives a woman a way to take positive action on behalf of her family, encouraging her to talk to God about her family. Each page includes a brief devotional, Scripture, and a prayer focused on a different quality or characteristic she wants family members to have"–Provided by publisher.
   Includes index.
   ISBN 0-7642-0190-5 (hardback : alk. paper)
   1. Grandmothers–Prayer-books and devotions–English. 2. Mothers–Prayer-books and devotions–English. I. Title.

BV4847.Y34 2006
242'.6431–dc22   2006003141

To God

*All that [I] have accomplished
you have done for [me].*

ISAIAH 26:12

❋

To Grandmothers

*Even when I am old and gray,
do not forsake me,
O God, till I declare your power
to the next generation.*

PSALM 71:18

❋

To my Mom

*I have not stopped giving thanks for you,
remembering you in my prayers.*

EPHESIANS 1:16

Contents

Introduction

Agrandmother's heart is not so different from a mother's heart—except that it has more people to love and to pray for. As a grandmother your most powerful influence will be the example you set for your family. Let that example be that you are a woman of prayer. Leave a legacy of prayer for your family so that it is clear that God is your source of all wisdom, strength, and hope.

A Grandmother's Guide to Praying for Her Family equips you with 260 prayers to pray specifically and intentionally for your family, covering all areas of life. These easy foundational prayers are just the beginning to greater conversations with God and for creating a heritage of prayer in your family.

Each prayer is rooted in and echoes God's perfect Word; each Bible verse sets forth one godly characteristic for building a family on the Rock, Jesus Christ. Between the Bible verse and the prayer is a brief devotion offering inspiration, instruction, or an idea to consider.

Page by page, this book provides simple prayers you can bring before the Lord, knowing not only that his Word is living and active, sharper than any double-edged sword, but that he promises his Word will not return to him empty, but will accomplish his purposes. Use *A Grandmother's Guide to Praying for Her Family* to get you started praying for your own family. Let God speak to you through each Bible verse and devotion and learn from him. Pray for faith and character for your family and establish a legacy of prayer that will touch generations to come.

Unless the Lord builds the house,
its builders labor in vain.

PSALM 127:1

Boldness

*Let us therefore approach
the throne of grace with boldness, so that
we may receive mercy and
find grace to help in time of need.*

HEBREWS 4:16 NRSV

Prayer is a great gift that provides direct access into the presence of God. Christ opened the way to come boldly to the throne of God at any time, in any place, with any words. Fearlessly unload your burdens and with great expectation receive mercy and grace to help in your time of need.

*Almighty God, with boldness
I pray for my family. Give mercy and
grace to my children and grandchildren in
their time of need. Amen.*

Devoted to Prayer

Devote yourselves to prayer,
being watchful and thankful.

COLOSSIANS 4:2

Devotion to prayer leads to an intimate relationship with God. Faithfulness to God through prayer is the greatest gift that you can pass down to your children and grandchildren. Start now to establish a legacy of prayer in your family.

❧

Living and Eternal God, grant that my
children and grandchildren
will be devoted to prayer,
being watchful for your
answers and thankful for
your blessings. Amen.

Pray Scripture

So is my word that goes out from my mouth: It will not return to me empty, but will accomplish what I desire and achieve the purpose for which I sent it.

ISAIAH 55:11

How should you begin to pray? Use Scripture as the foundation for your prayers and seek God's will for your family expressed in his own words. Claim God's promise that his Word will not return empty, but will accomplish all he desires for your family.

Mighty Lord, thank you for the assurance that your Word expressed for my family will not return to you empty, but will accomplish what you desire and achieve the purpose for which you sent it. Amen.

Blessed With Children

*Sons are a heritage from the Lord,
children a reward from him.*

PSALM 127:3

The Lord is so great to bless you with children and grandchildren. Thank God each day for everyone in your family. Tell your children and grandchildren that they are God's reward to you.

*Thank you, Lord, for your reward to me of
children and grandchildren. Amen.*

Welcoming

And whoever welcomes a little child like this in my name welcomes me.

Matthew 18:5

How wonderful to spend time with your grandchildren! Welcome your precious grandchildren with open arms. Help them to gain an understanding of their heavenly Father through the love you show to them.

Heavenly Father, may my welcome of my grandchildren teach them to welcome everyone in your name. Amen.

Tell the Next Generation

Even when I am old and gray, do not forsake me, O God, till I declare your power to the next generation.

Let it be your lifetime mission to declare God's power, majesty, and love to the next generation. Begin today to profess the message of Jesus Christ to your grandchildren. Tell the story of God's glory through song, storytelling, and Scriptures.

O God, when my husband and I are old and gray, grant us the strength to continue to declare your power to the next generation. Amen.

Proclaim the Gospel Clearly

*Pray that I may proclaim
[the gospel] clearly, as I should.*

COLOSSIANS 4:4

You don't have to be a well-trained preacher to tell the gospel story. Make it simple for your grandchildren. Clearly state that God loves them so much that he sent Jesus to rescue them from their sins and gives them life with him forever if they are sorry for their sins and obey him.

*Jesus, Lamb of God, let the simple gospel
story penetrate the hearts of my
grandchildren so they too may proclaim
the gospel clearly. Amen.*

Born Again

*You should not be surprised at
my saying, "You must be born again."*

JOHN 3:7

With the birth of each grandchild,
you joyfully celebrate a new life.
God also celebrates the spiritual birth of
new believers who confess their sins and
put their trust in Jesus as Lord and Savior.
Have you given your heavenly Father cause
for celebration?

*Gracious Father, wake up in my family
members a need to be born again
by repenting and putting their
trust in you. Amen.*

Childlike Faith

*Let the little children come to me! Never
send them away! For the Kingdom of
God belongs to [people] who have hearts
as trusting as these little children's.*

LUKE 18:16 TLB

Your grandchildren are precious reminders
of the relationship God desires to have
with you. As your grandchildren look to
you in total trust and love, so you are
to look to your heavenly Father. When you
seek God, he will never send you away.

*Jesus, increase my family's childlike trust
in you. Inspire each one to cling to
you in love and reliance as they mature in
years and grow in faith. Amen.*

Careful

Be very careful, then, how you live—
not as unwise but as wise,
making the most of every opportunity,
because the days are evil.

EPHESIANS 5:15-16

The time you spend with your grandchildren is treasured. Make the most of every opportunity to introduce them to Jesus. Collect favorite Bible verses together, create a CD of beloved Bible stories to be heard when you are not close-by, and connect life events to God's presence in your lives.

Eternal Lord, help me to make the most of every opportunity to teach my grandchildren about you so they may be careful and wise in how they live. Amen.

Godly Foundation

Unless the Lord builds the house,
those who build it labor in vain.

PSALM 127:1 RSV

With a few Lego blocks and a deck of cards you can illustrate to your grandchildren the importance of making Christ their faith foundation. Snap the Legos in place and the structure is secure, lean cards together and the house easily collapses. A faith built on the Lord rests eternally secure.

Lord, help my grandchildren to build their
faith with you as their foundation.
Strengthen their faith with building blocks
of prayer, praise, and promise. Amen.

Mature

*Don't be childish in your understanding
of these things. Be innocent as
babies when it comes to evil, but be
mature and wise in understanding
matters of this kind.*

1 CORINTHIANS 14:20 NLT

Ignite a spark of faith by reading the Bible
with your grandkids, teaching them about
God and his desires for them, and modeling
a daily prayer life, seeking the Holy Spirit's
wisdom. Guide them to maturity in their
relationship with Jesus Christ.

❧

*Mighty God, grant my grandchildren
the desire for a mature faith
and the wisdom to follow
you. Amen.*

Hot Faith

I know what you do, that you
are not hot or cold.
I wish that you were hot or cold!

REVELATION 3:15 NCV

If you or your loved ones are not red hot for the Lord, don't be satisfied. A lukewarm faith deceives only the person who has it— God knows it is no faith at all. Challenge your family to replace spiritual pride with repentance, self-reliance with Christ-dependence, and busyness with quiet time spent in devotion and prayer.

Lord, stoke my family's faith so
it is red hot for you. Amen.

Diligent

You have commanded
your precepts to be kept diligently.

PSALM 119:4 NRSV

We diligently put at the top of our priority list those things most important to us. Is God at the top of your list? Do you earnestly read the Bible, praise God in daily prayer, and confess your failure to obey his commands?

❧

O Lord, excite my children and
stepchildren, their spouses,
and my grandchildren to diligently obey
you and to keep your precepts. Amen.

Love

Love is patient; love is kind; love is not
envious or boastful or arrogant or rude.
It does not insist on its own way; it is
not irritable or resentful; it does not
rejoice in wrongdoing, but rejoices in
the truth. It bears all things, believes all
things, hopes all things, endures all things.

1 Corinthians 13:4-7 NRSV

Remember, God is love and the source
of all love. Inscribe these Bible verses
on your heart and teach them to your
family through word and deed so they will
know how to love as God intended. Now
go, love abundantly.

Lord God, help my family
to know your love and to live in love
with each other. Amen.

Encourage Others

*But encourage one another daily, as long
as it is called Today, so that none of you
may be hardened by sin's deceitfulness.*

HEBREWS 3:13

We all need a little encouragement
each day. Provide a smile, a laugh, or
a hug. Especially encourage your husband
each morning and celebrate together God's
grace for another day.

*Jesus, thank you for this day and for my
husband. Help us to encourage each
other daily so we are not hardened by sin's
deceitfulness but rather
delighted with your gift
of life. Amen.*

Protected

But let all who take refuge in you be glad; let them ever sing for joy. Spread your protection over them, that those who love your name may rejoice in you.

Psalm 5:11

Place your grandchildren in God's hands for his daily and eternal protection. Seek God for shelter from all that can harm the body and soul. Rejoice that God claims each grandchild as his own and knows each by name.

Mighty Lord, spread your protection over my grandchildren. Let them take refuge in you and be glad. Amen.

Noble Character

A wife of noble character...her children arise and call her blessed; her husband also, and he praises her.

PROVERBS 31:10, 28

If only we could choose wives for our grandsons! In some ways we can by being an example of a wife of noble character. Display integrity, honesty, and excellence for your grandson so he recognizes important virtues of a godly woman and wife.

Precious Savior, guide my grandson to desire a godly woman for a wife so their children may call her blessed and he may also praise her. Amen.

Respectful

Show respect for everyone.

1 Peter 2:17 nlt

Respect is foundational to any relationship. It builds trust, love, and self-esteem. Respect each of your loved ones by keeping your promises, deferring to family decisions, and validating each person's worth as a child of God.

*Jesus, guide my family
to show respect for everyone. Amen.*

Pure Mind

Set your minds on things above,
not on earthly things.

COLOSSIANS 3:2

I t is hard to set your mind on things above
when the things below are so close by.
Ungodly attitudes, actions, and appearances
are as near as the TV and pop culture
magazines. You must make deliberate
choices to avoid the sins of this world and
to actively pursue the things of God.

Holy Lord, protect my family
from the evils of this world. Guide them to
make godly choices and to set their minds
on things above. Amen.

Praise

*Let everything that
has breath praise the Lord.*

PSALM 150:6

Embrace your children and glorify
God! Wrap your arms around your
grandchildren and give thanks for life,
for love, for liberty. Praise the Lord!

*May my sons and daughters, sons-in-law
and daughters-in-law, grandsons and
granddaughters burst forth in praise to you,
Almighty and Everlasting God. Amen.*

Know God's Will

Be joyful always; pray continually;
give thanks in all circumstances, for this
is God's will for you in Christ Jesus.

1 Thessalonians 5:16-18

I n a complicated world, teach your
grandchildren the simplicity of God's will.
Model for them a joyful spirit, pray together
frequently, and give thanks often. Live God's
will day by day in the presence of your family.

Lord Jesus, give my grandchildren the
understanding that your will for them is to
be joyful, prayerful, and thankful at all
times and in all circumstances. Amen.

Alert

Be self-controlled and alert. Your enemy
the devil prowls around like a roaring
lion looking for someone to devour.

1 PETER 5:8

S in can be so subtle that its gradual
advance into your life goes unnoticed
until it is ready to devour you. Make no
mistake about it, the devil is real and
desires your soul. Be alert to sin's deception
and sound the warning to your family.

Mighty Lord, help my children to be
self-controlled and alert so they are not
lulled into temptation and sin; protect my
grandchildren from cleverly disguised evils
ready to devour
them. Amen.

Godly Sorrow

*Godly sorrow brings repentance
that leads to salvation.*

2 CORINTHIANS 7:10

Don't trivialize God's forgiveness.
God doesn't want a rote confession,
but rather a broken and contrite heart.
Understand the seriousness of your sinful
condition and you will experience godly
sorrow that leads to salvation.

*Merciful Savior, lead my children
and grandchildren to express godly sorrow
for their sins to receive forgiveness and
eternal life. Amen.*

Pray in the Spirit

*But you, dear friends, build yourselves
up in your most holy faith
and pray in the Holy Spirit.*

JUDE 20

We don't always know how to pray
for our families—our children, their
spouses, our grandchildren, and their
sometimes blended families. Take comfort
that God knows all. By praying in the Holy
Spirit, the Spirit brings before the Father
your family's needs that you cannot express
or even know.

*Holy Spirit, build my loved ones up
in the most holy faith and meet their needs
that only you fully know. Amen.*

Honor Marriage

*Marriage should be honored by all,
and the marriage bed kept pure,
for God will judge the adulterer and
all the sexually immoral.*

HEBREWS 13:4

Infidelity has infected many marriages.
The healing process begins by acknowledging
sin, seeking forgiveness, and honoring the
marriage vows. If marital infidelity has
sickened your family, trust that in God's
strength a new life of faithfulness can begin.

*Holy God, strengthen my children's
marriages so they may
honor their marriage
vows and keep
the marriage bed
pure. Amen.*

Know God Works
for Good

---

*And we know that in all things
God works for the good of those
who love him, who have been called
according to his purpose.*

ROMANS 8:28

God can bring good from a bad situation. In Jesus, God brought life from death, salvation from damnation. Love God with abandonment, be obedient to his call, and trust in his eternal perspective.

*God, when my family runs into defeats and
disappointments, assure them that
in all things you work for the good of those
who love you and have been
called according to your purpose. Amen.*

Cheerful Giver

*Each of you must give as you
have made up your mind,
not reluctantly or under compulsion,
for God loves a cheerful giver.*

2 CORINTHIANS 9:7 NRSV

Grandchildren bring out the joy of giving in us. Our love for them ignites a passion to give to them. Does your love for God instill that same passion to give to God?

*Gracious God, prompt my grandchildren
to be cheerful givers to those in need,
knowing that you are
the Great Provider. Amen.*

Crave God's Word

*Like newborn babies, crave pure
spiritual milk, so that by it you may
grow up in your salvation.*

1 PETER 2:2

Like new grandbabies who crave milk, so
you are to crave the Word of God.
Christian growth does not occur without
the nourishment offered in the Bible.
Don't starve your faith by failing to read
your Bible.

*Lord Jesus, stir up a craving
in my children and grandchildren to daily
feed on your Word by reading and
studying the Bible. Help them to grow up
in their salvation. Amen.*

Saved

*Turn to me and be saved, all you
ends of the earth; for I am God,
and there is no other.*

Isaiah 45:22

Have each of your loved ones turned
to the Lord to be saved? Do they
understand that there is no other god who
can save them from their sins? Do you?

*Lord God, turn each of my family members
to you to be saved. Give them the
assurance that you are the only true God
and there is no other. Amen.*

Fishers of Men

*Jesus called out to them,
"Come, be my disciples, and I will show
you how to fish for people!"*

MARK 1:17 NLT

Teach your grandchildren to be fishers of people. Take them fishing in a lake or the bathtub (with pretend fish) to illustrate that God has outfitted them to fish for unsaved souls. Excite your grandchildren to reel in those who do not know Christ by inviting them to Sunday school or youth group.

Jesus, when you say, "Come," help my grandchildren to follow you and learn to be your disciples. Amen.

Listen to God

This is my beloved Son, and I am fully pleased with him. Listen to him.

MATTHEW 17:5 NLT

Do you spend time in prayer without pausing to listen to the Holy Spirit speaking to your heart? Do you tell God what he should do without listening to what he wants you to do? God the Father tells us to listen to Jesus. Are you listening?

Almighty Lord, hush my children and their children so they will listen to your beloved Son. Amen.

Responsible

*For we are each responsible
for our own conduct.*

GALATIANS 6:5 NLT

When you are wrong, do you admit it?
When you have made a poor choice,
do you accept the consequences? Seek
forgiveness and make restitution when your
irresponsible conduct has brought injury
to another.

*Merciful God, guide my children
to demonstrate responsibility so that
their children will learn to be responsible
for their own conduct as well. Amen.*

Choose to Serve God

---

*You must choose for yourselves today
whom you will serve.... As for me and
my family, we will serve the Lord....*

JOSHUA 24:15 NCV

If your child is married to an unbeliever,
choosing to serve God as a family may be
difficult for them. Support your children so
they may honor God and their spouse.
Continue to stand firm in the faith,
relentlessly pray for the unbeliever, and in
love exhibit a Christ-filled life of service to
the Lord.

❧

*Almighty God, lead my children
and their spouses to choose today to serve
Jesus all their lives. Amen.*

Hopeful

*But blessed are those who trust
in the Lord and have made the Lord
their hope and confidence.*

JEREMIAH 17:7 NLT

Christian hope is not founded on one's
own merit. All have sinned, so Christian
hope rests solely on Jesus' blood and
righteousness. If you do not have that hope,
ask the Holy Spirit to fill your life and
receive the assurance that comes when you
surrender your life to God.

*Almighty God, be my family's hope
and confidence from this day forth and
forevermore. Amen.*

Moral

Therefore, get rid of all moral filth
and the evil that is so prevalent
and humbly accept the word planted
in you, which can save you.

James 1:21 nlt

It is hard to reject what society has so readily accepted. Pray for the desire to turn off popular TV shows that dishonor God and to stop going to movies that portray all kinds of immoral filth. Help your grandchildren learn to be discerning in the choices they make.

❀

Holy God, guide my grandchildren
to rid themselves of all immoral filth and
the evil that is so prevalent around
them and to humbly accept your Word
that can save them. Amen.

Love Your Wife

*However, each one of you also
must love his wife as he loves himself.*

<small>EPHESIANS 5:33</small>

Wives desire love from their husbands.
Love is shown in many ways but
especially by providing attention, affirmation,
and affection. Teach your sons and grandsons
how to express love in words and deeds.

❧

*Loving God, guide my sons
and grandsons to love their wives as they
love themselves. Amen.*

Holy

You must be holy, because I am holy.

1 PETER 1:16 NCV

The status of being a grandmother sets you apart from the majority of the population. So too being a Christian distinguishes you from most of the world. As God can have no part of sin, so you too are to be distinct from the world's sinful ways.

Holy God, fill me with the desire to be holy as you are holy, that my grandchildren will see you in me. Amen.

Joyful

Make a joyful noise to God,
all the earth; sing the glory of his name;
give to him glorious praise.

PSALM 66:1-2 NRSV

What a joy to hold a new grandbaby! What a joy to watch your children become godly parents. Make a joyful noise to God for his many blessings.

Glorious God, thank you for the
joy my children and grandchildren bring
into my life. Amen.

Peacemaker

Blessed are the peacemakers,
for they will be called children of God.

MATTHEW 5:9 NRSV

Amother-in-law is frequently portrayed as stirring up trouble. However, God calls us to be peacemakers. Make an effort to bring peace to your in-laws' house by respecting their family rules and traditions.

❦

Father, bring peace and love to my
daughter-in-law's house so that all
who enter may be blessed as peacemakers
and called children of God. Amen.

Qualified

Giving thanks to the Father, who has qualified you to share in the inheritance of the saints in the kingdom of light.

COLOSSIANS 1:12

Praise God that you don't have to qualify for heavenly benefits. You are fully vested in the righteousness of Jesus the moment you believe. Your "work" for the kingdom is in grateful response to Christ's atoning work on the cross.

Thank you, Lord Jesus,
for qualifying my family to share
eternity with you. Amen.

Led by the Spirit

For all who are led by the
Spirit of God are children of God.

ROMANS 8:14 NLT

Playing a simple game of follow the
leader with the grandkids can provide an
important life lesson. Explain that you are a
child of God and every day you are led by
the Spirit of God. Help them see the Holy
Spirit's leadership through you.

Holy Spirit, lead my grandchildren
day by day and help them
to rely on you for direction. Amen.

Kept From Stumbling

*And now, all glory to God, who is able
to keep you from stumbling, and who
will bring you into his glorious presence
innocent of sin and with great joy.*

JUDE 24 NLT

Like a grandmother's hand reaching out
to keep a small child from falling,
so too God reaches out to keep you from
stumbling in your faith. Grab hold of
God's hand and marvel at his tender care.
Be God's hand for your grandchildren and
keep them from stumbling in the faith.

*Faithful God, help my grandchildren
and children reach out to you to keep from
stumbling in the faith. Amen.*

Do Not Exasperate

Fathers, do not exasperate your children.

EPHESIANS 6:4

Parenthood can be exasperating. Focus on the joys, look to God for strength, and love unsparingly. Help your husband and sons deal patiently with their children.

Heavenly Father, guide the fathers in my family not to exasperate their children. Amen.

Called to Belong

*And you also are among those
who are called to belong to Jesus Christ.*

ROMANS 1:6

Adopted children have been called to
belong in their new families. You too
have been adopted—into God's family.
As God has called you to belong to Jesus
Christ and welcomes you into his family,
you too can welcome adopted children and
introduce them to the Christian family.

*Lord, assure my adopted grandchildren
that you have called them
by name to belong to Jesus Christ. Amen.*

Fellow Citizens

*Consequently, you are
no longer foreigners and aliens,
but fellow citizens with God's people and
members of God's household.*

Ephesians 2:19

As your children's girlfriends and boyfriends become wives and husbands, they become fellow citizens in your household. They are family. Similarly, God has taken you in as family, as a member of his household.

*Thank you, God, for my children's spouses
who are now part of our family. Give us all
thankful hearts for being fellow citizens
and members of your household. Amen.*

Heirs to Eternal Life

*So that, having been justified
by his grace, we might become heirs
having the hope of eternal life.*

TITUS 3:7

Do you wish that you could leave a grand inheritance to your children? You can. Lead them to a personal relationship with Jesus as their Lord and Savior and they will be heirs to eternal life.

Gracious God, bring each of my family members to a saving faith in Christ so they may inherit eternal life with you. Amen.

Truthful

A good man hates lies; wicked men lie constantly and come to shame.

PROVERBS 13:5 TLB

The devil is the master of lies. Align yourself with the God of Truth and speak the truth. Help your grandchildren to understand that the truth honors God and will keep them from shame.

❧

Almighty God, instill in my grandchildren a hate for lies and a love for truth. Amen.

Redeemed

In him we have redemption through his blood, the forgiveness of sins, in accordance with the riches of God's grace.

EPHESIANS 1:7

A redeemed coupon converts from a worthless piece of paper into valuable savings. Similarly, through Christ you have been redeemed, converted from a worthless sinner into a forgiven, righteous child of God. You now have eternal value.

Lord Jesus, thank you for the redemption we have through your death and resurrection. Help my children and their families to live for you as your redeemed children. Amen.

Merciful

*Be merciful, just as
your Father is merciful.*

<small>LUKE 6:36</small>

Mercy is forgiving when undeserved,
excusing when not merited, and
giving when not entitled. God in his mercy
spared you from hell. If you have accepted
God's mercy, how can you not be merciful
to others?

*Merciful Father, grant that my
grandchildren will learn to be merciful
as you are merciful so they will
extend mercy to each other
and to all people. Amen.*

Christian

*Yet if any of you suffers as a Christian,
do not consider it a disgrace, but glorify
God because you bear this name.*

1 PETER 4:16 NRSV

Troubles are inevitable for Christians
because Christian values conflict with
the world's values. You will experience
rejection for taking a biblical stand. Rejoice
that the troubles you encounter are because
you won't deny God or renounce his ways.

*Lord Jesus, strengthen my
family's faith when they suffer as
Christians. Let them glorify
you because they bear your
name. Amen.*

Kind to the Needy

He who despises his neighbor sins, but
blessed is he who is kind to the needy.

PROVERBS 14:21

Sometimes the needy are so close they
make us feel uncomfortable. At other
times they are so far away we forget about
them. Open your eyes to the needs of those
around you and to those whom God puts
on your heart so you might extend God's
kindness and his provision.

Gracious God, help my children and
grandchildren to understand your kindness
so they might likewise be kind to
all in need in their community and
throughout the world. Amen.

Restored Health

For I am the Lord, who heals you.

EXODUS 15:26

Our hearts ache when a loved one is sick. Entrust your family to the Lord's care and healing. Pray fervently for restored health of both body and soul.

❦

Lord, comfort my family
with the assurance that you are
the one who heals. Restore the health
of my loved one. Amen.

Spirit-Filled

Do not quench the Spirit.

1 Thessalonians 5:19 NRSV

Busyness, pride, and selfishness quench the Spirit. Are you too busy to read the Bible, too proud to depend on God, or too selfish to be concerned about another's salvation? If you have quenched the Spirit, repent and ask God to fill you with his Holy Spirit right now.

Holy Spirit, I pray that my loved ones will desire your presence and not turn you away. Amen.

Put God First

In everything you do, put God first,
and he will direct you and
crown your efforts with success.

PROVERBS 3:6 TLB

I f your day planner is filled in and God is
squeezed out, then it is time to adjust
your priorities. The busier you are, the
greater your need to spend time with God
in prayer and the Scriptures. Put God first
in your daily schedule and be wonderfully
amazed how God works out all the details.

Lord God, in all they do,
help my children and grandchildren to put
you first and hold on to the promise
that you will direct them and crown their
efforts with success. Amen.

Meditate

*But his delight is in the law
of the Lord, and on his law he meditates
day and night.*

PSALM 1:2

The Bible contains God's love letters to you. Pore over those letters, meditate on his love, and dwell on his message. Delight in all that he is telling you and obediently act on what he is calling you to do.

*Eternal God, may I pass your love letters
on to my children and grandchildren
so they too may delight in your Word and
meditate on you day and night. Amen.*

Live to See Grandchildren

And may you live
to see your children's children.

PSALM 128:6

You are blessed with grandchildren. What joy and love they bring into your life! Praise God that you have lived to see your children's children.

Thank you, most gracious God,
that I have lived to see my grandchildren.
Bless our time together. Amen.

Repentant Prodigal

*Return to the Lord your God, for he is
gracious and compassionate, slow to
anger and abounding in love,
and he relents from sending calamity.*

JOEL 2:13

Teenagers have a way of showing their
independence by rejecting God and
family values. If you have such a teenage
grandchild, show him or her God's grace
and compassion. Love unconditionally,
talk frequently, and pray continually.

*Sovereign Lord, through your grace and
compassion may my prodigal grandchild
repent and return to you. Amen.*

A Heart to Know God

I will give them a heart to know me,
that I am the Lord.

JEREMIAH 24:7

God has given each of us a heart to know him. Help your grandchildren to find that heart. Guide them to know God intimately through the Scriptures, worship, and prayer.

Heavenly Father, thank you for giving
us hearts that seek to know you.
Lead my grandchildren into a saving
relationship with you. Amen.

Reject Witchcraft

Do not practice divination or sorcery....
Do not turn to mediums or seek out
spiritists, for you will be defiled by them.

LEVITICUS 19:26, 31

Witchcraft exists today. Young people dabbling in the occult often get caught in its snare. Warn your grandchildren that God detests witchcraft because it defiles them and turns them away from him.

Jesus, shield my grandchildren
from the evils of witchcraft and sorcery.
Strengthen their faith in you. Amen.

Walk in Truth

*I have no greater joy than to hear
that my children are walking in the truth.*

3 JOHN 4

What a blessing to know loved ones
who have accepted Jesus as their Savior!
What anguish knowing there are still some
who reject him. Keep praying for the
salvation of the unbelievers and sing praises
to God for those who walk in the truth.

*Gracious God, lead my whole family
to know you as their Lord and Savior and
to walk in your truth. Amen.*

Wisdom

If any of you lacks wisdom,
he should ask God, who gives generously
to all without finding fault, and
it will be given to him.

JAMES 1:5

Wisdom and knowledge are different.
Someone can be highly educated but
not wise in making sound judgments or
given to deep understanding. To be wise in
the things of God for your family, ask God
for wisdom and he will give generously.

Lord, I pray that my family
will boldly seek your wisdom and learn
to discern your ways. Amen.

Imitators

Be imitators of God.

Ephesians 5:1

How proud you can be when a child or grandchild chooses to go to your alma mater or follows your career path. Clearly your excitement for your school or career was an influence. Has your love for Christ influenced your family to follow in your spiritual footsteps?

Holy God, invigorate my loved ones to be imitators of you. Amen.

Gracious

Let your speech always be gracious,
seasoned with salt, so that you may
know how you ought to answer everyone.

COLOSSIANS 4:6 NRSV

Season your speech with God's truths
that flavor your grandchildren's lives.
Graciously share your faith with your
grandchildren. Start talking about Jesus when
they are young, so as they grow, it will be
natural and easy to discuss faith questions.

Guide my grandchildren to
know you personally so they will speak
graciously as well as sensibly to
everyone who
seeks answers.
Amen.

Show No Favoritism

As believers in our glorious
Lord Jesus Christ, don't show favoritism.

JAMES 2:1

You may see some of your grandchildren
more frequently and know them better
than others. The fastest way to crush a
grandchild's spirit and stir up jealousy in
your family is to favor one grandchild over
another. Show no favoritism, but instead
imitate the love that Jesus equally bestows
on all.

Dear Jesus, help my family and me not
to show favoritism and give us the ability to
lovingly treat all people equally. Amen.

Know the Creator

*I praise you because I am fearfully
and wonderfully made; your works are
wonderful, I know that full well.*

PSALM 139:14

Society does not embrace God's creation
story. Counter the culture by explaining
to your grandchildren how God made their
wonderfully complex and orderly bodies.
Praise God together for his hand in every
detail of life.

*Almighty God, Creator of all, give my
grandchildren insight into your marvelous
creation and how fearfully and wonderfully
you have made them. Amen.*

One With God

*I pray also for those who will believe in
me through [the disciples'] message,
that all of them may be one, Father, just
as you are in me and I am in you.
May they also be in us so that the world
may believe that you have sent me.*

JOHN 17:20-21

After several years of marriage, spouses
know each other so well they almost
act as one. Jesus prayed that we would be
one with God. Are you spending time with
God so that you know him well enough to
be one with him?

*Jesus, help my husband and me
to know you so well that we will be one
with you and so radiate your love
to our grandchildren. Amen.*

Belong to God

*The person who belongs to God
accepts what God says.*

JOHN 8:47 NCV

Y ou cannot pick and choose Bible
principles you agree with and ignore
the rest. You either take the whole Bible as
God's inspired Word or you don't believe
in the God of the Bible. The person who
belongs to God accepts his Word.

❋

*Father, I pray that my children,
their spouses, and their children will
accept your Word as truth and
thereby belong to you. Amen.*

Earnest

*Those whom I love I rebuke
and discipline.
So be earnest, and repent.*

REVELATION 3:19

Y ou can't fool God. He knows your
heart and whether you are genuinely
sorry for your sins. If you have never come
to the Savior with great sorrow for your
sins, do so now.

*Lord God, thank you for loving my family
so much that you rebuke and
discipline them. Bring them to earnest
repentance for their sins. Amen.*

Flee Youthful Desires

Flee the evil desires of youth,
and pursue righteousness, faith, love and
peace, along with those who call on
the Lord out of a pure heart.

2 TIMOTHY 2:22

Whether due to immaturity, peer pressure, or Satan, your grandchildren will encounter evil desires. Help ground your grandchildren in God's standards so they will recognize ungodly desires. Counsel them to flee temptations by running to God for strength to pursue righteousness.

Invincible God, prompt my grandchildren
to flee the evil desires of youth, and help
them to pursue righteousness, faith, love,
and peace, along with all those who call on
the Lord out of a pure heart. Amen.

The Mind of Christ

But we have the mind of Christ.

1 CORINTHIANS 2:16

Young or old, educated or not, everyone who yields their life to Christ can have the mind of Christ. Be united with Christ's concern for the unsaved. Share the salvation message with those who are still unsure what to believe and why.

Lord, give my loved ones the mind of Christ so they can share your concern and love for the unsaved. Amen.

Selflessness

Do nothing out of selfish ambition
or vain conceit, but in humility consider
others better than yourselves.

PHILIPPIANS 2:3

Mothers readily put their children's needs before their own. They selflessly give up their time, energy, and the last piece of cake. Tell your daughters and daughters-in-law what a great job they are doing with their children and shower them with praise for their selflessness.

Lord, I pray my daughters and
daughters-in-law will see selflessness and
humility in me. Amen.

Justified

Therefore, since we are justified by faith,
we have peace with God
through our Lord Jesus Christ.

ROMANS 5:1 NRSV

Grandmothers naturally try to fix
problems for their family. A lot of
advice is given in hopes of providing a
solution. Be sure your family knows that Jesus
is the answer to the eternal problem of sin
and that all who believe are justified by faith.

Bless my family with the
peace of justification received through faith
in Jesus Christ. Amen.

Intercessor

*I looked in vain for anyone who would
build again the wall of righteousness
that guards the land, who could stand in
the gap and defend you from
my just attacks, but I found not one.*

EZEKIEL 22:30 TLB

When was the last time you took a stand for righteousness? Have you pursued God on behalf of someone else? Do you stand in the gap pleading with God for your family's righteousness and salvation?

❦

*Lord, make intercessors of
my saved family members to stand in the
gap for the unsaved. Amen.*

Seek God

*But seek first his kingdom and
his righteousness, and all these things
will be given to you as well.*

MATTHEW 6:33

D o you play hide-and-seek with your
grandchildren? Remember the squeals
of delight when they find you? Are you
helping them to seek God and experience
the thrill of discovering him?

*Lord God, guide my grandchildren
to seek first your kingdom and to
obediently serve you. Amen.*

Treasured Possession

*For you are a people holy to the
Lord your God. Out of all the peoples on
the face of the earth, the Lord has chosen
you to be his treasured possession.*

<small>DEUTERONOMY 14:2</small>

Your grandchildren are the crowning
jewels of your blessed life. They are also
God's treasured possession. Frequently tell
your grandchildren how precious they are to
you and to God.

❦

*Lord, remind me to tell my grandchildren
at each visit and with every phone call
or e-mail how much I love them
and that they are your treasured possession,
loved with an everlasting love. Amen.*

Ready

Therefore you also must be ready,
for the Son of Man is coming
at an unexpected hour.

MATTHEW 24:44 NRSV

You have spent the better part of life getting ready. You have prepared for school, career, marriage, children, grandchildren, and retirement. Are you prepared to meet Jesus face-to-face, and is your family ready too?

Jesus, I pray my loved ones
will be ready to meet you at an
unexpected hour. Amen.

Inspired

*All scripture is inspired by God and
profitable for teaching, for reproof,
for correction, and for training in
righteousness, that people of God may be
complete, equipped for every good work.*

2 TIMOTHY 3:16 NRSV

Parents often wish they had an owner's
manual for raising their children. God
did provide such a manual. Let your adult
children know that the Bible provides
everything needed to raise godly children.

❧

*God, help the parents of my grandchildren
to understand your Word and to use it
for teaching, for reproof, for correction, and
for training in righteousness,
so that their children may be complete,
equipped for every good work. Amen.*

Prepared

Always be prepared to give an answer to
everyone who asks you to give the reason
for the hope that you have.

1 PETER 3:15

Your extended family may consist of
unbelievers, seekers, or new believers of
the faith. Do not be unprepared for probing
or hostile questions. In preparation, study
the Bible, memorize God's Word, and pray
for wisdom.

✳

Holy God, I pray that each believer
in my family will be well prepared to give
an answer to all who ask the reason
for the hope they have. Amen.

Proud of Family

You have such a place in our hearts that we would live or die with you. I have great confidence in you; I take great pride in you. I am greatly encouraged; in all our troubles my joy knows no bounds.

2 CORINTHIANS 7:3-4

Reveal your heart to your family. Tell your children how proud you are of them in raising their own children and convey your confidence in your grandchildren to make God-pleasing choices. Be encouraged by God's presence in their lives.

*Lord God, thank you for my family.
I am so proud of each one
and encouraged by their love for you.
Even in our troubles, my family brings me
great joy. Thank you. Amen.*

Integrity

I know, my God, that you test the heart and are pleased with integrity.

<small>1 CHRONICLES 29:17</small>

The best way to teach integrity is to live it. When you are in the wrong, confess it; when you have been overpaid, return it; when you have damaged something, replace it. If you don't have integrity 100 percent of the time, you don't have integrity.

Holy God, cultivate integrity within my children so they in turn can teach their children that you are pleased with integrity. Amen.

Bring Good News

*How beautiful on the mountains are the
feet of those who bring good news,
who proclaim peace, who bring good
tidings, who proclaim salvation.*

ISAIAH 52:7

The announcement of a birth,
homecoming, or job promotion is
eagerly welcomed. Even more beautiful is
the news of a family member accepting
Christ as their Savior. Be the beautiful feet
that bring the good news of Jesus to those
who do not know him yet as Lord.

*Lord Jesus, motivate the believers
in my family to proclaim the good news
of salvation to those who have not
yet accepted Jesus as their Savior. Amen.*

Healed

*He heals the brokenhearted and
binds up their wounds.*

Place all your hurts and brokenness at
the foot of the cross. Let Jesus heal your
mind, body, and soul. Trust in God's loving
concern and healing touch.

*Healing God, heal the brokenhearted
in my family and bind their
wounds through the blood of Jesus. Amen.*

Beautiful

*It is not fancy hair, gold jewelry, or fine
clothes that should make you beautiful.
No, your beauty should come from
within you—the beauty of a gentle and
quiet spirit that will never be destroyed
and is very precious to God.*

1 Peter 3:3-4 ncv

P hysical beauty changes over time.
Be assured, God does not look at the
outside appearance, but rather at the beauty
of a gentle and quiet spirit. If you fully
trust in Christ, you are beautiful.

*Creator God, give my granddaughters
the assurance that true beauty
is not physical beauty, but
the inner beauty of a gentle and quiet
spirit that trusts in you. Amen.*

Living Sacrifice

In view of God's mercy …
offer your bodies as living sacrifices,
holy and pleasing to God.

ROMANS 12:1

Your selfless acts of love toward your children and grandchildren are living sacrifices, holy and pleasing to God. Let your living sacrifices extend to the rest of the community as well. Use your talents, time, and treasures to serve God's people and to exemplify God's love.

Jesus, use my family in your
service. Let our lives
be a living sacrifice,
holy and pleasing
to you. Amen.

Shielded by God's Power

Through faith [you] are shielded
by God's power until the
coming of the salvation that is ready
to be revealed in the last time.

1 Peter 1:5

The grandkids may pretend they are fighting aliens and put up their invisible force field to ward off enemy attack. Their play provides a great analogy. Spiritual dangers do surround us and through faith we are shielded by God's power until the coming of salvation.

All-powerful God, shield my grandchildren
from evil until you come again. Amen.

Watchful

*Keep a close watch on all you do
and think. Stay true to what is right
and God will bless you and
use you to help others.*

1 TIMOTHY 4:16 TLB

When you are baby-sitting your
grandchildren, you must watch their
every move so they don't get hurt. You also
must watch the example you are setting for
them. Are you honoring God with your
language, TV viewing, and reading material?

*Savior, keep my children and
grandchildren watchful for
spiritual danger, courageous
to do what is right, and
useful to you to help
others. Amen.*

Remember the Sabbath

*Remember the Sabbath day
by keeping it holy.*

EXODUS 20:8

If your grandchildren do not have
Christian parents, you have a vital role in
introducing the children to Christ. Ask
their parents if you can take the grandkids
to church. Teach your grandchildren about
setting aside a day to worship God with the
fellowship of believers.

*Righteous Lord, help my children
and grandchildren to remember to put you
first and to make Sunday a holy day
to worship you. Amen.*

Eager to Serve

Feed the flock of God; care for it willingly, not grudgingly; not for what you will get out of it, but because you are eager to serve the Lord.

1 PETER 5:2 TLB

Moms feed their flock of children and care for them willingly. They do it out of love, not for what they will get in return. So too we are to care for God's people because we love God and are eager to serve him.

Lord, create in my daughters and daughters-in-law an eagerness to serve you by serving their families and others. Amen.

Jesus' Friend

*I have called you friends, for everything
that I learned from my Father
I have made known to you.*

JOHN 15:15

It is a joy to be a grandmother and a friend
to your grandchildren. Sharing a good
laugh, playing games, and listening to each
other's stories bring contentment and delight.
Take pleasure in knowing that Jesus has
also called you friend; share his friendship
with your grandchildren.

*Beloved Jesus, be my
grandchildren's best friend. Amen.*

Thankful

It is good to give thanks to the Lord,
to sing praises to your name, O Most High;
to declare your steadfast love in the
morning, and your faithfulness by night.

PSALM 92:1-2 NRSV

Everything we have comes from God. Yet how often we forget to give thanks. Today as you thank God for all things, tell your husband and family how thankful you are that God brought them into your life.

❋

O Most High, thank you for my husband
and family and the life you have
given to us. Bind us together as we declare
your steadfast love and faithfulness
all day long. Amen.

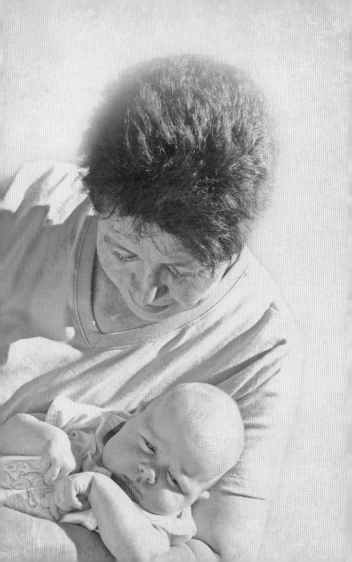

Avoid Arguments

Again I say, don't get involved
in foolish arguments, which only upset
people and make them angry.

2 Timothy 2:23 tlb

Remember, your children are adults,
and you are not the parent to your
grandchildren even though your influence
can be powerful. Your relationship with
your children and grandchildren is more
important than winning a minor point
regarding a problem not yours to solve.
Foolish arguments, no matter who starts
them, produce few winners.

O Lord, keep my children and me
from foolish arguments that only upset us
and make us angry. Amen.

Perfect

Aim for perfection.

2 CORINTHIANS 13:11

Perfection is impossible if you are aimed in the wrong direction. Jesus was perfect. Aim your family toward him.

❧

Jesus, I pray my children and grandchildren will turn in your direction so they are aimed for perfection. Amen.

Accountable to God

*So then, each of us will
give an account of himself to God.*

ROMANS 14:12

Mature Christian friends can help you
in your Christian walk. Form an
accountability group with friends you can
trust to hear your struggles and to provide
strong Christian counsel. Let them prepare
you for the accounting you will someday
give directly to God.

❧

*Holy God, give my family an
understanding that every thought,
word, and deed must be accounted for
to you. Guard their hearts
and minds until that day. Amen.*

Speak Boldly

*Enable your servants to
speak your word with great boldness.*

ACTS 4:29

Why is it so hard to talk about Jesus?
Ask God to enable you to boldly
speak about salvation offered through
Christ. Practice your boldness with your
family and then reach out to others.

*Precious Jesus, enable me to speak your
Word with great boldness to my loved ones
and then to others. Amen.*

Obey God, Not Man

We must obey God rather than men!

ACTS 5:29

Obeying God means living a life pleasing to God. Within your house, set boundaries of acceptable godly conduct. Let no vile talk be spoken, no immoral behavior sanctioned, and no illegal business conducted.

Lord God, strengthen my grandchildren's desire to obey you rather than others. Amen.

Generous

All goes well for those who are generous,
who lend freely and
conduct their business fairly.

PSALM 112:5 NLT

It is easy to be generous with your grandchildren. Relate your generosity to God who freely gave his Son for the sins of the world. Help your grandchildren learn to lend freely and serve others fairly in response to God's generosity to them.

Father, help my grandchildren
to be generous, lend freely,
and conduct their
business fairly. Amen.

Worshipful

Come, let us bow down in worship,
let us kneel before the Lord our Maker.

PSALM 95:6

When the grandkids are visiting, take them to church and show them how to worship God. Teach them about the God of the Bible and what Jesus has done for them. Encourage your grandchildren to worship God each day, glorifying him in thought, word, and deed.

Lord our Maker, nurture in my grandchildren a desire to kneel before you in worship each day. Amen.

Temple of the Holy Spirit

*Do you not know that your body
is a temple of the Holy Spirit, who is in
you, whom you have received from God?
You are not your own.*

1 CORINTHIANS 6:19

What a joy to watch grandchildren run and jump and play; their bodies full of energy and life. Tell them that their bodies are the temple of the Holy Spirit that lives within them. Teach them to honor God with their bodies.

*Holy Spirit, help my grandchildren
to treat their bodies as a temple for you,
your holy dwelling place. Protect them
from drugs, alcohol, and anything
that damages the body. Amen.*

Press On

*Forgetting what lies behind and
straining forward to what lies ahead,
I press on toward the goal for the prize of
the heavenly call of God in Christ Jesus.*

PHILIPPIANS 3:13-14 NRSV

Don't dwell on the past. It cannot be changed or relived. Instead, press on toward the goal of eternity with God and start pleasing him from this day forward.

*Jesus, help my dear family to forget
what lies behind and press on to
that heavenly goal to be with you. Amen.*

Worthy

*Only, live your life in a manner worthy
of the gospel of Christ.*

PHILIPPIANS 1:27 NRSV

Jesus went from town to town ministering
to the people. In the end, he gave his life
for their sins and yours. Are you patterning
your life after Christ's example of love and
forgiveness?

*Loving Lord, I ask that my family
will desire to live their lives in a manner
worthy of you. Amen.*

Pursue Peace

*Let us then pursue what makes
for peace and for mutual upbuilding.*

ROMANS 14:19 NRSV

Grandmothers can be a safe haven for
grandchildren living in homes
disrupted by marital conflict or divorce.
Make your home a place of rest and peace.
Bring God's unconditional love to each
child and build each up emotionally and
spiritually.

*Almighty God, bring peace to my
children's homes. Help my children and
grandchildren to pursue peace
and build each other up with words of
encouragement and love. Amen.*

Teach Children About God

Only be careful, and watch
yourselves closely so that you do not
forget the things your eyes have seen or
let them slip from your heart....
Teach them to your children and to
their children after them.

DEUTERONOMY 4:9

Your love for God is a treasure to pass on to your children and grandchildren. Share God's precious truths. Keep talking about God with your family so you don't forget what your eyes have seen or your heart has experienced.

Immortal God, help me to teach
my children and grandchildren how to
know you intimately. Amen.

Image of God

So God created human begins in his image.
In the image of God he created them.
He created them male and female.

GENESIS 1:27 NCV

Your teenage and young adult grandchildren may be struggling to know where they fit in. Societal pressures may be trying to transform them into something they are not. Let your grandkids know that God made them and loves them just as they are.

Almighty God and Creator,
help my grandchildren to appreciate that
you created them in your image. Amen.

Humble

*They should be gentle and
show true humility to everyone.*

TITUS 3:2 NLT

Humility is understood when you stand
at the cross of Christ and comprehend
that it was your sins that crucified your Lord.
Your worth stems from Christ alone; all
self-righteousness and pride must be cast
aside. In light of Christ's sacrifice, show true
humility to all.

*O Lord, in a nation of excess,
help my children and grandchildren to
recognize that self-worth comes
only from you so they may show true
humility toward all people. Amen.*

Undivided Heart

*Teach me your way, O Lord,
and I will walk in your truth; give me
an undivided heart,
that I may fear your name.*

PSALM 86:11

You cannot cut your heart in half and survive. Similarly, you cannot divide your heart between God and some earthly desire and survive spiritually. Give your whole heart to God and live.

❧

*Sovereign God, teach my family
your way so they may walk in your truth.
Give them an undivided heart
that they may fear your name. Amen.*

Pursue Righteousness

But you, man of God, flee from all this,
and pursue righteousness, godliness,
faith, love, endurance and gentleness.

1 TIMOTHY 6:11

The computer opens a door to a wealth of information; it also opens the door to the sin of pornography. Remind your sons and grandsons of God's standards. Warn them to flee all sin and pursue righteousness.

Holy God, strengthen my sons and
grandsons to flee from all sin and to pursue
righteousness, godliness, faith,
love, endurance, and gentleness.
Amen.

Heaven Focused

When I look at your heavens, the work of
your fingers, the moon and the stars
that you have established; what are
human beings that you are mindful of
them, and mortals that you care for them?

<small>PSALM 8:3-4 NRSV</small>

O n a clear night gaze at the moon and
the stars with your grandchildren.
Exclaim the magnificence of God's creation
and how he spoke it into existence from
nothing. Let the starry heavens be a lifelong
reminder of God's incredible love for your
grandchildren.

Heavenly Father, when my grandchildren
see the majesty of your universe,
may they praise you that you are mindful
of them and care for them. Amen.

Walk in Obedience

And this is love: that we
walk in obedience to his commands.

2 John 6

Wasn't it fun to watch your babies learn to walk? You rejoiced with each step and lovingly encouraged greater distances. So it is with God who cheers you on as you walk with him in obedience and inspires you to go the distance in your life with him.

Holy Lord, support my children's walk
with you and guide them
to obey your commands. Amen.

Motivated

Give yourself wholly to [your gifts],
so that everyone may see your progress.

Be your grandchildren's motivator.
Cheer them on in school, sports, and
the Christian faith. Stay in touch so that
your godly motivation will inspire them
to wholeheartedly use their spiritual gifts to
the glory of God.

Jesus, I ask that my grandchildren
will be motivated to give themselves wholly
to their spiritual gifts to be used
in service for you. Amen.

Considerate

Husbands, in the same way be considerate as you live with your wives.

1 PETER 3:7

Consideration is thinking about the needs of others before your own. Sometimes we are more considerate to strangers than to our own families. Let your actions show consideration to all your family members.

Sovereign God, thank you that my husband is a godly model for our sons to learn to be considerate as they live with their wives. Amen.

Submissive

Wives, in the same way be submissive
to your husbands so that,
if any of them do not believe the word,
they may be won over without words
by the behavior of their wives.

1 PETER 3:1

If you are living with an unbelieving
spouse, he may tire of preachy speech in
an effort to convert him to the faith. Win
your husband over to Christ by honoring
and respecting him in private and in
public. Speak of Christ's love and draw him
to God through your godly conduct.

Christ Jesus, let my daughters' behavior
win over their husbands to
love you without reserve. Amen.

Faithful Servant

Well done, good and faithful servant!

MATTHEW 25:21

You cannot earn God's grace, but you can reject it. Accept God's unmerited forgiveness by repenting of your sins and joyously serving him. Go and tell others about Jesus Christ and eagerly anticipate God's heavenly welcome, "Well done, good and faithful servant!"

Heavenly Father, prompt my family to faithfully serve you so when they are welcomed into your kingdom you will say, "Well done, good and faithful servant!" Amen.

Follow the Way

*Jesus answered, "I am the way
and the truth and the life."*

JOHN 14:6

Today's prevalent view that all roads lead
to heaven really opens a wide gate on a
broad road to hell. Jesus said he alone is the
way and the truth and the life. If you don't
believe in Jesus, you are on the wrong road.

❧

*Jesus, convict and assure
my family that you alone are the way and
the truth and the life. Amen.*

Harvest Worker

*The harvest is plentiful, but the
workers are few. Ask the Lord of the harvest,
therefore, to send out workers
into his harvest field.*

Luke 10:2

Look around at your grandchildren. The
harvest is plentiful. Tell your faith
story to your grandchildren and proclaim
God's faithfulness in your life.

❧

*Lord of the harvest,
raise up my grandchildren to be harvest
workers for you. Amen.*

Stand Mature

*Stand mature and fully
assured in everything that God wills.*

COLOSSIANS 4:12 NRSV

Watching children and grandchildren mature is delightful. It is fun to be a part of each age and stage of development. Take part in their spiritual development as well by encouraging them to meditate on God's Word, memorize Scripture, and meet with fellow believers.

*Help my children and grandchildren
to stand mature and fully assured
in your will, O God. Amen.*

Foolish Heart

*The fool says in his heart,
"There is no God."*

PSALM 53:1

Hold a newborn grandbaby in your arms and witness another of God's precious miracles. Watch the sunset at the ocean's edge and experience God's creation. Only a fool would say there is no God.

*Creator God, our world is
evidence of your living presence. Amen.*

Do Not Follow the Crowd

Do not follow the crowd in doing wrong.
EXODUS 23:2

S in can creep into our lives so subtly that without much thought we are watching morally depraved TV shows, accepting living arrangements outside of marriage, and playing golf on Sunday mornings. Just because everybody is doing it doesn't make it right. Read your Bible so you know what God expects, and stop following the crowd.

❧

Lord, protect my grandchildren from
peer pressure to do wrong.
Direct them to follow you. Amen.

Speak Timely Words

Everyone enjoys giving good advice,
and how wonderful it is to be able to
say the right thing at the right time!

Timely words can bestow blessings,
encourage hearts, and mend relationships.
The phrases "I love you," "You can do it,"
or "I am sorry" are always welcome. Seek
God for wise counsel to give to your family
at the right time.

Gracious God, give each family member
the right words to be
spoken at the
right time. Amen.

Do All in God's Name

And whatever you do, in word or deed,
do everything in the name
of the Lord Jesus, giving thanks to God
the Father through him.

<small>COLOSSIANS 3:17 NRSV</small>

When you woke up this morning,
God gave you another day of life.
Whether the day will be ordinary or
extraordinary, live for God and give thanks.
Let others around you see that your zest for
life stems from your love for the Lord.

Lord Jesus, in everything we do,
help my family and me to bring honor to
your name and to gratefully
serve you in word and deed. Amen.

Strengthen Your Heart

Strengthen your hearts,
for the coming of the Lord is near.

JAMES 5:8 NRSV

Diet and exercise help keep your heart strong. Get your heart in shape for the Lord and be ready for him to come again. Nourish your soul on God's Word, exercise your faith muscles with fellow believers, and lift up your heart in prayer.

Almighty God, strengthen the hearts
of my family members and keep them
firmly in the faith until you
come again. Amen.

Conscious of Sin

*Through the law we
become conscious of sin.*

ROMANS 3:20

No matter how good a person you are,
do you understand your sinfulness?
Review the Ten Commandments (Exodus
20) and you will become conscious of your
sin. Acknowledging your sin is the first step
to understanding your need for Christ and
his forgiveness.

*Jesus, bring to my family
members' minds their sins so they may come
to you in repentance and put their
confidence in you. Amen.*

Controlled by
the Holy Spirit

*You, however, are controlled not
by the sinful nature but by the Spirit,
if the Spirit of God lives in you.*

ROMANS 8:9

Don't be a backseat driver with God.
Let him be in control. Surrender
your life into his care and let the Spirit of
God direct you.

*Holy Spirit, teach the parents
of my grandchildren to relinquish control
of their lives to your Spirit so that
my grandchildren can learn by
their example. Amen.*

Fulfilled

The Lord will fulfill his purpose for me.
PSALM 138:8

God's purpose for you may have been revealed in a moment of life or a life of moments. Sometimes to see God's work in your life you need only to look at your children and grandchildren. Until the Lord calls you home, continue to seek his guidance, be attentive for his answer, and be ready to respond.

Lord, give to my family a glimpse of your purpose for them and the assurance that it will be fulfilled. Amen.

Righteous

The righteous will live by faith.

ROMANS 1:17

Your commitment to Christ is evidenced by how you live your life for him. Are you just putting in pew time at church? Or are you making a difference in someone's life, knowing that Jesus' righteousness has made a difference in yours?

🌹

Redeemer Lord, you have made us righteous. Help my family to live by faith and in faith reach out to others who need to hear the good news of Jesus. Amen.

Forgiving

*If someone does wrong to you,
forgive that person
because the Lord forgave you.*

COLOSSIANS 3:13 NCV

Marriage provides ample opportunity
to practice forgiveness. Don't keep
track of each other's wrongs. Forgive each
other as the Lord forgave you.

*Merciful Savior, remind my husband
and me never to grow
weary of forgiving each other. Amen.*

Example

Set the believers an example in speech and conduct, in love, in faith, in purity.

1 TIMOTHY 4:12 NRSV

What does your life say about your love for God? Do people even know you are a Christian? Set an example in all you do that clearly declares your devotion to God.

Lord Jesus, teach my children and grandchildren to set an example in speech and conduct, in love, in faith, and in purity. Amen.

Model of Good Deeds

*Show yourself in all respects
a model of good deeds.*

<small>TITUS 2:7 RSV</small>

Faith without action is worthless. Provide more than words of compassion to the downtrodden. Mirror Jesus' love by feeding the hungry, visiting the sick, and being a friend to the friendless.

*Holy God, inspire my family
to show themselves in all respects a model
of good deeds. Amen.*

Tell Family About God

Moses told his father-in-law
about everything the Lord had done.

Exodus 18:8

Sometimes talking about God to your family is hard. It is important that we not exclude those we love most. Seek God for just the right words to tell your extended family about everything the Lord has done for you.

Sovereign God, embolden the believers
in my family to tell others
everything you have done. Amen.

Right Words

*Pray also for me, that whenever
I open my mouth, words may be given
me so that I will fearlessly
make known the mystery of the gospel.*

EPHESIANS 6:19

A re you afraid to speak up for the Lord
because you don't know what to say?
Are your children or grandchildren fearful?
Pray for each other to have just the right
words to fearlessly make known the gospel
of Jesus.

*Gracious God, give my loved ones
and me just the right words so that when
needed, we will fearlessly speak
about your love and salvation. Amen.*

Cheerful

*A cheerful look brings joy to the heart,
and good news gives health to the bones.*

PROVERBS 15:30

S mile. Bring joy to the heart of a store
clerk, a neighbor, or a grandchild.
Pass along the good news of Jesus to bring a
smile to everyone you meet each day.

❧

*Lord, let each of my loved ones be cheerful,
knowing that you have given them
eternal life. Help them to bring the good
news to those who do not know you. Amen.*

Merciful to Doubters

Be merciful to those who doubt.

JUDE 22

D oubts are a normal part of growing in faith. Walk through the doubts with a doubter and assure them that God's grace cannot be undone.

Lord, weed out the doubts
in my family so they will be merciful
to others who doubt. Amen.

Sustained in God

*Even to your old age and gray hairs
I am he, I am he who will
sustain you. I have made you and I
will carry you; I will sustain you
and I will rescue you.*

ISAIAH 46:4

What a privilege to grow old! We are living examples of God's sustenance. Tell the stories of how God carried you through difficult days, rescued you when you were lost in sin, and sustained you in your faith.

*Almighty God, sustain my children
in the faith, even until
they are old and gray. Amen.*

Do Not Grumble

You are not grumbling against us,
but against the Lord.

EXODUS 16:8

Did you know grumbling to yourself or others is really grumbling against the Lord? God has given you life so that you may glorify him. Catch yourself before you grumble and look to God with thanksgiving for all he has given to you.

Lord God, giver of life, keep my
grandchildren from grumbling.
Help them to be thankful for your many
blessings, especially the eternal gift
of your Son, Jesus. Amen.

Submit to One Another

*Submit to one another
out of reverence for Christ.*

EPHESIANS 5:21

Both male and female alike are to depend on each other and make Christ their model. Respect and honor one another. Let your behavior honor Christ.

Lord Jesus, as you loved the church so we seek to model your love. Help the married couples in my family to submit to each other out of reverence for you. Amen.

Trust

Trust in the Lord forever, for the Lord,
the Lord, is the Rock eternal.

ISAIAH 26:4

I f you believe God is real and what the
Bible says is true, why is it so difficult to
trust him? Depend wholeheartedly on him
to direct your future, your finances, and
your family. Have confidence that God,
who created you and the universe, knows
what is best for you.

❧

I pray, dear God, my family,
immediate and extended, will trust
in you always. Amen.

Kind

Be kind and loving to each other, and forgive each other, just as God forgave you.

EPHESIANS 4:32 NCV

Sometimes kindness evades everyday family life. Make it a point to be kind to your loved ones even when they may not be kind to you. Teach forgiveness by extending it as God did to you.

❋

Jesus, help my children, stepchildren, and grandchildren to be kind and to forgive one another. Amen.

Compassionate

*As God's chosen ones, holy and
beloved, clothe yourselves
with compassion, kindness,
humility, meekness, and patience.*

COLOSSIANS 3:12 NRSV

God has chosen you to be
compassionate. Are you concerned
about people's eternal needs as well as their
physical needs? Does your compassion
reach out to the unsaved?

*O God, clothe each of my dear family
members in compassion, kindness,
humility, meekness, and patience. Amen.*

Know God

Be still, and know that I am God.

PSALM 46:10

Life in the fast lane makes us feel important and needed. However, the fast track often bypasses God and our quiet time with him. Learn to slow down enough to include God on life's journey so you may travel into eternity with him.

God Almighty, slow us down.
Lead my children and their families to
find quiet times to be still,
and know that you are God. Amen.

Call on the Lord

*Anyone who calls on the Lord
will be saved.*

ROMANS 10:13 NCV

If you make it a habit to call on God in
the good times, you will naturally call
on him in the bad times too. Talk to God
throughout your day. Make it your practice
to be in fellowship with your Savior at
all times.

*Lord, create in my loved ones
the desire to call upon your name
and be saved. Amen.*

Transformed

*Do not be conformed to this world,
but be transformed by the renewing of
your minds, so that you may
discern what is the will of God—what is
good and acceptable and perfect.*

ROMANS 12:2 NRSV

S ociety chips away at your resolve little
by little. Before you know it, your ideas
and values have conformed to the ways of
the world. Renew your mind by examining
the Bible and knowing God's good,
acceptable, and perfect will so you will be
transformed into God's way of thinking.

*Almighty God, protect my family from
conforming to the unholy standards of this
world. Renew their minds so they may
discern your will. Amen.*

Eagerly Waiting

*So Christ, having been offered
once to bear the sins of many,
will appear a second time, not to deal
with sin, but to save those who are
eagerly waiting for him.*

HEBREWS 9:28 NRSV

Everyone has an appointment with
Jesus, although the scheduled time is
unknown. With eager anticipation start each
day ready to meet Jesus. In preparation,
invite the Holy Spirit into your daily life
and pray for those who don't yet know
your Savior.

*Jesus my Savior, I pray you will find my
sons and daughters, grandsons and
granddaughters eagerly waiting for you to
come again on the last day. Amen.*

Servant Leader

Whoever wants to become great
among you must serve
the rest of you like a servant.

MATTHEW 20:26 NCV

God doesn't define greatness by the number of people you command but rather by the way you serve. There are many kingdom duties that simply require humble obedience. Follow your Savior to the cross and be willing to do the uncelebrated jobs.

Savior, teach my children and their
families that if they want to
be leaders, they must be servants,
tending to the needs of others. Amen.

Self-Control

So we should not be like other people
who are sleeping, but we
should be alert and have self-control.

1 Thessalonians 5:6 NCV

I f you don't watch out, you get lazy and
undisciplined in your relationship with
God. However, you need to stay alert
because the devil seeks your soul. Don't be
found slumbering in your faith because you
lacked the self-control to spend time with
Jesus each day.

Father, keep my family from spiritual
slumber; help them to be alert to
Satan's deceptions and to maintain
self-control to daily follow you. Amen.

Declare God's Glory

Declare his glory among the nations,
his marvelous deeds among all peoples.

PSALM 96:3

Grandchildren are such a blessing!
Declare God's glory to your grandkids
with every hug given and received. Express
God's marvelous deed of giving life and love.

Living Lord, help me tell my grandchildren
about you and encourage them
to declare your glory among
the nations and your marvelous deeds
among all people. Amen.

Confident

*For the Lord will be your confidence and
will keep your foot from being snared.*

PROVERBS 3:26

Life is full of changes and the future
uncertain. Nevertheless, if your
confidence is in the Lord, you can approach
each day without fear. Your salvation
is secure.

*Dear God, give my grandchildren
sure footing. Help them to put
their confidence in you alone. Amen.*

Mustard-Seed Faith

*I tell you the truth, if you have faith
as small as a mustard seed....
Nothing will be impossible for you.*

MATTHEW 17:20

As you introduce your grandchildren to
Jesus, you are planting seeds of faith.
Even if you are a new Christian and afraid
you don't know very much, teach your
grandchildren what you do know and learn
more together. Let the mustard seeds of
faith in Christ blossom together.

*Jesus my Savior, help me to
plant seeds of faith. Nurture each
grandchild's faith and mature it to
bear fruit for you.
Amen.*

Keep the Faith

I have fought the good fight, I have finished the race, I have kept the faith.

2 TIMOTHY 4:7

Christian college students face many faith challenges from peers, professors, and philosophies. It is a fight to come out of college with a higher spiritual GPA than upon entering. Teach your college-bound children and grandchildren to defend the faith by knowing what they believe and why.

Faithful God, equip those in my family attending college to defend the faith; encourage them to finish the race and empower them to keep the faith. Amen.

Live and Die
for Christ

*For to me, living is Christ
and dying is gain.*

PHILIPPIANS 1:21 NRSV

Jesus reigns in both life and death because of his victory on Calvary. Bring comfort to those who are fearful of death's grip. Assure them of eternal life to all who repent and put their trust in Christ. Give glory to God in your living and your dying.

✿

*Righteous Jesus, thank you
for conquering death. Take away my
children's fear of my death or theirs.
Help us bring glory to you in
our living and our dying. Amen.*

Salvation in Jesus

There is salvation in no one else!
There is no other name in all of heaven
for people to call on to save them.

ACTS 4:12 NLT

Don't let your grandchildren grow up
thinking that it doesn't matter what
you believe as long as you sincerely believe
it. Nothing could be further from the truth.
Salvation is only found in Jesus; there is no
other name under heaven by which you can
be saved.

Jesus my Savior, you alone provide salvation.
Draw my children and grandchildren
close to you so they know
in whom to put their
trust. Amen.

In Anger Do Not Sin

"In your anger do not sin":
Do not let the sun go down while
you are still angry.

EPHESIANS 4:26

Life is too short to spend it mad at someone. Resolve your differences quickly. Be the first to repair any broken relationship, whether it is your fault or not.

✿

Redeemer God, thank you for your
gift of forgiveness. Help my family to settle
their disputes quickly so that
by day's end there is no anger. Amen.

Carry Others' Burdens

Carry each other's burdens.

GALATIANS 6:2

Think of a heavy duffel bag with two handles. Your child or grandchild could struggle to carry it alone, or you could each grab a handle and share the load. The load isn't so bad when shared by two.

❧

Sovereign Christ, you carried our load of sin. Strengthen my family to carry each other's burdens to lighten life's load. Amen.

Pray for Others

So Peter was kept in prison,
but the church was
earnestly praying to God for him.

ACTS 12:5

Addictive substances or behaviors become a prison to those involved. If you have a loved one locked into an addiction, encourage your family members to earnestly pray for that one's release. Let the addict know that you are bringing him or her before God and pleading for new life.

Merciful God, have mercy on
my loved ones who are imprisoned by
addiction. Turn their destructive behavior
to dependence upon you. Amen.

All Is Possible
With God

For nothing is impossible with God.

LUKE 1:37

Wow! Nothing is impossible with God.
Go, believe, and expect a miracle.

Lord, when I am fearful remind me
that nothing is impossible with you. Amen.

Tell of God's Deeds

We will tell the next generation the
praiseworthy deeds of the Lord,
his power, and the wonders he has done.

PSALM 78:4

Start seeing God in everyday events.
Look for answers to your prayers, God's
protection in your life, and the wonders he
is doing within your family. Point out the
workings of God to your grandchildren so
together you can praise his name.

Mighty God, teach my grandchildren
to look for evidence of you in
their lives and to praise you for the
wonders you have done. Amen.

Light

You are the light of the world.

MATTHEW 5:14

In darkness people lose their way. Be a light on the path to Jesus. Invite an unbeliever to your church, share a Bible verse with a friend, and encourage a new neighbor to join your small group Bible study.

Almighty God, thank you for Jesus, our eternal light. Guide my family to shine your gospel light into the lives of unbelievers. Amen.

Come and See

"Come," [Jesus] replied, *"and...see."*

JOHN 1:39

When a grandchild says, "Come and see," we enthusiastically follow, welcoming some cherished sight or accomplishment. Jesus has also said, "Come and see." Are you eagerly following him to gladly take in all he wants to show you?

❦

Jesus, when you say, "Come and see"
to my loved ones, spur each
to gladly welcome and follow you. Amen.

No Buts

I will follow you, Lord; but first let me...

LUKE 9:61

No excuses. No delays. Follow Jesus right away.

❧

Lord Jesus, I pray that no excuse or delay will prevent my children or grandchildren from following you. Amen.

Disciple

So no one can become my disciple
unless he first sits down and counts his
blessings—and then renounces
them all for me.

LUKE 14:33 TLB

The cost of discipleship is putting
everything second to Christ. Jesus is to
be first in your marriage, your family, your
career, and your finances. How are you
doing as a disciple?

Jesus, nothing is more prized
than following you. I pray my children
and grandchildren will eagerly
become your disciples. Amen.

Every Thought Captive

We demolish arguments and
every pretension that sets itself up
against the knowledge of God,
and we take captive every thought to
make it obedient to Christ.

2 CORINTHIANS 10:5

Do not be deceived into thinking that truth is relative. God's Word is absolute truth. Take captive every thought that distorts biblical truth and make it conform to the teachings of Christ.

Lord, protect my children and
grandchildren from Satan's deception and
teach them to take captive every thought
to make it obedient to Christ. Amen.

Cling to Good

Hate what is evil; cling to what is good.

ROMANS 12:9

The Bible clearly states that some things are not only wrong but also evil. God calls us to hate what is evil and cling to what is good. Warn your family against compromising or excusing away God's truths.

*Righteous God,
help my family hate what is evil and
cling to what is good. Amen.*

Ears That Listen

Let anyone with ears listen!

MATTHEW 11:15 NRSV

Listening is a hard skill to master because too often we just want to tell others, as well as God, how it is and what we want. Take time today to be quiet before the Lord and listen. Take some time to listen to your family too.

Lord, open my children's ears so they will listen to their spouse and to you. Amen.

Silence Ignorant Talk

*For it is God's will that by
doing right you should silence the
ignorance of the foolish.*

1 PETER 2:15 NRSV

Christians champion biblical values.
It is in your words and deeds that
your faith is proved genuine to unbelievers.
Let your good deeds silence the criticism
of unbelievers.

*Lord Jesus, strengthen my grandchildren to
stand up for you when challenged by
people who resist knowing you. Help them
to do what is right and thereby silence the
ignorant talk of foolish people. Amen.*

Test Everything

Test everything. Hold on to the good.

1 Thessalonians 5:21

You know that not everything is as it appears. Test every idea, value, and social issue against biblical principles so you are not conned by a humanistic worldview and false teachers. Help your family hold on to God's good and perfect ways.

Jesus, point my family to your Word
so they may test everything
and hold on to the good. Amen.

Store Treasures
in Heaven

*Do not store up for yourselves treasures
on earth...but store up for yourselves
treasures in heaven.... For where your
treasure is, there your heart will be also.*

Matthew 6:19-21 nrsv

Years of earthly treasures are sure to be
found in your closets, basement, or
attic. Let these "treasures" remind you of
the fleeting pleasures of anything not having
eternal value. Store up heavenly treasures by
visiting the sick, clothing the poor, and
feeding the hungry.

*Precious Jesus, as the materialism of
this world contends for my family's attention,
grant to them strength to focus
on storing up treasures in heaven. Amen.*

Loving

We love because he first loved us.

1 John 4:19

God so loved the world that he sacrificed his perfect Son in payment for every sin. Jesus loved you as a sinner, but died for you to be a saint. How can you not love others in response?

*Loving Father, guide my husband
and me to reach out to each new addition
to our family in love because you first
loved us. Amen.*

Wear Whole Armor

Put on the whole armor of God,
so that you may be able to stand against
the wiles of the devil.

EPHESIANS 6:11 NRSV

The devil is deceptive. Put on the whole armor of God so you are ready to fight daily temptations. Arm yourself with Christ's righteousness by repenting of your sins, hold the shield of faith by inviting the Holy Spirit into your life, and wield the Word of God by knowing Scripture by memory.

Invincible God, clothe my dear family
with your armor so that they may
withstand the wiles of the devil. Amen.

Grow in Grace

*But grow in the grace and knowledge of
our Lord and Savior Jesus Christ.*

2 PETER 3:18 NCV

Help faith take root. Tell your
grandchildren about Jesus, read Bible
stories together, and teach them how to pray.
Take an active part in your grandchildren's
spiritual growth.

*Savior, cultivate my grandchildren's
faith so they will grow
in grace and knowledge of you. Amen.*

Discern What Is Right

*And this is my prayer: that your love
may abound more and more
in knowledge and depth of insight,
so that you may be able to discern what
is best and may be pure and
blameless until the day of Christ.*

PHILIPPIANS 1:10

Some behavior that was unacceptable in years past is now permissible. Society's changing values stand in opposition to God's unwavering standards. Know God's Word so you clearly understand the difference between right and wrong.

*Father, I pray that my loved ones will
always see clearly the difference
between right and wrong, and be inwardly
clean at Christ's return. Amen.*

New Creation

*So if any one is in Christ, there is a new
creation: everything old has passed
away; see, everything has become new!*

2 CORINTHIANS 5:17 NRSV

Skip the liposuction, skin peels, and Botox
that claim to make you a new person.
Go directly to Christ and become a new
creation. Watch your old sinful desires pass
away as you set your sights on eternal beauty.

*Beautiful Savior, lead my daughters,
daughters-in-law, and granddaughters to
become new creations in you and
to live their lives for your glory. Amen.*

Please God

We are not trying to please men but God,
who tests our hearts.

1 Thessalonians 2:4

Politically correct speech may please the
listener but offend God. Remember, you
are only accountable to God. Stress to your
family the importance of pleasing God by
holding on to his eternal truths in the face
of society's pressure to appease everyone.

Holy God, shield my children, their spouses,
and my grandchildren from trying
to please others more than you. Amen.

Obey Government

*Obey the government, for God is
the one who has put it there.
There is no government anywhere that
God has not placed in power.*

ROMANS 13:1 TLB

You may have a political opinion different
from other family members. Don't let
differences of opinions affect your
relationships. Remember, we all must
respect the government God has established
and work within it to bring change.

✳

*God, help my family remember
that you are the one who has established all
governments. Amen.*

Clear Minded

The end of all things is near.
Therefore be clear minded and
self-controlled so that you can pray.

1 PETER 4:7

Your memory may get fuzzy about some events, but remain clear minded about Jesus' death and resurrection in payment for your sins. Jesus restored your relationship with God so that you can come boldly into his presence through prayer and be obedient to his call. The end of all things is near, so do not delay in surrendering your life to Jesus.

Holy God, keep my family clear minded
and self-controlled so they can
pray until you come again. Amen.

Patient

Be patient with everyone.

1 THESSALONIANS 5:14

Impatience abounds on the roads, in checkout lines, and in daily life. When you become agitated or experience another's impatience, cling tightly to God's desire for you to be patient with everyone. Show your grandchildren godly patience.

Almighty God, teach my grandchildren
to be patient with everyone,
and let me set the example. Amen.

Boastful in the Lord

Let the one who boasts, boast in the Lord.

2 Corinthians 10:17 NRSV

Grandmas love to boast about their grandchildren. What an opportunity to give glory to God for the work he is doing in your family. Take the moment to shine the spotlight on God for his handiwork.

❦

Gracious God, give to my grandchildren and children the understanding that all things come from you so that all boasting is in you. Amen.

Stand Firm

*But he who stands
firm to the end will be saved.*

MATTHEW 24:13

The older you get the clearer it becomes
that change is inevitable. However, God
is the same yesterday, today, and tomorrow.
Don't abandon the Word of God for the
changing culture; stand firm to the end and
be saved.

*Lord, strengthen each of my family
members to stand firm in the faith until
the end of time. Amen.*

Guard Your Tongue

*He who guards his mouth and
his tongue keeps himself from calamity.*

PROVERBS 21:23

Grandmothers gush about their
grandchildren. Don't let your words
build up one grandchild at the expense of
another. Guard your tongue and keep out
of trouble.

*Eternal Lord, guard my family
from tearing down others or
spewing out hurtful words. Amen.*

Live on God's Word

Jesus answered, "It is written:
'Man does not live by bread alone,
but on every word that
comes from the mouth of God.'"

MATTHEW 4:4

While junk food has become a major food group in many families, don't let junk religions fill your grandchildren. As you are able, be sure they know that the God of the Bible is the only true God, who offers forgiveness of sins and eternal life. Serve them the Bread of Life.

❧

Jesus, may my dear grandchildren
crave your Word every day and grow in faith,
knowing you are the Bread of Life. Amen.

Draw Near to God

Draw near to God
and he will draw near to you.

JAMES 4:8 RSV

People who eagerly approach others easily make friends. God is waiting for you to approach him. He is ready to begin and mature a wonderful relationship with you if you will just draw near to him.

Heavenly Father, encourage
my children and their spouses to draw
near to you, knowing you desire
to draw near to them. Amen.

Never Waver

*Abraham never wavered in believing
God's promise. In fact,
his faith grew stronger, and in this
he brought glory to God.*

ROMANS 4:20 NLT

Are you growing closer to God? Looking back over the years, how have you matured spiritually? If your faith is wavering, get reacquainted with God by spending time in prayer, praise, and the Scriptures.

*Almighty God, prompt my family to
examine their spiritual growth.
If their faith is wavering, inspire them
to spend more time with you
so they may glorify you. Amen.*

Well Behaved

*Even a child is known by his actions,
by whether his conduct is pure and
right.*

PROVERBS 20:11

Grandmas delight in their grandchildren and often focus on the positive. Your encouragement of godly conduct encourages more of the same. Help your grandkids understand that being well behaved is pleasing to you and to God.

*Heavenly Father, create a desire in my
grandchildren to be well behaved.
Give them a desire to
be known as your children by their
pure and right actions. Amen.*

Do Right

*So let us not grow weary in doing what
is right, for we will reap
at harvest time, if we do not give up.*

GALATIANS 6:9 NRSV

Exhaustion, busyness, and worldly
values are Satan's ways to lull you into
making ungodly choices. When you don't
have the energy to stand for what you know
to be right, keep your eyes on Jesus, who
endured the cross to save you from an
eternity in hell. Let God's grace motivate
you to keep doing what is right.

*Lord Jesus, strengthen my dear
family's faith so they will not
grow weary in doing what
is right. Amen.*

Fruit of the Spirit

*By contrast, the fruit of the Spirit
is love, joy, peace, patience,
kindness, generosity, faithfulness,
gentleness, and self-control.*

GALATIANS 5:22-23 NRSV

Does the Holy Spirit live within you?
The presence of the Spirit is evident
by love, joy, peace, patience, kindness,
generosity, faithfulness, gentleness, and
self-control. If you are lacking in these
characteristics, ask the Holy Spirit to dwell
in you today.

*O God, fill my children and their families
with your Spirit, so that they will
manifest your fruit in their lives. Amen.*

Gentleness

Let your gentleness be evident to all.

PHILIPPIANS 4:5

Men like to appear strong and tough. Roughhousing with the kids is fun; however, children enjoy tender moments with their dad as well. Remind the men in your family to balance their manliness with their children by letting their gentleness be evident to all.

O Lord, let my sons' gentleness
be evident to all and
thereby bring glory to you. Amen.

Work Hard

Work hard and cheerfully at all you do, just as though you were working for the Lord and not merely for your masters.

Colossians 3:23 TLB

Look at every task as an opportunity to work for the Lord. Let your work be an act of worship to your heavenly Master, who gives eternal wages. Then you can work hard and cheerfully no matter what job you are doing.

Help the breadwinners in my family, Lord, to work hard and cheerfully because they are working for you and not merely for others. Amen.

Alive in Christ

*I know your works; you have a name
of being alive, but you are dead.
Wake up, and strengthen what remains
and is on the point of death.*

Revelation 3:1-2 NRSV

As a Christian, you can get so busy
doing church-related activities that
you lose sight of God. In fact, busyness
may make you feel godly while your
relationship with God may be far from
intimate. Be alive in Christ rather than in
your busyness for him.

❧

*Christ Jesus, awaken my family
to be alive in you. Strengthen their faith
so that they put their trust in you
and not in their deeds. Amen.*

Strong in the Faith

Be strong in the faith, just as you were taught, and always be thankful.

COLOSSIANS 2:7 NCV

Spiritual "muscles" will weaken if they are not used. Build up your family's faith by encouraging family devotions, discussing faith issues with your husband and children, and e-mailing your Bible insights to your grandchildren. Be strong in the faith.

Mighty God, keep my children and grandchildren strong in the faith, just as they have been taught, and to always be thankful. Amen.

Matched With a Believer

Do not be mismatched with unbelievers.
For what partnership is there
between righteousness and lawlessness....
Or what does a
believer share with an unbeliever?

2 Corinthians 6:14-15 NRSV

You know firsthand the joys and difficulties of marriage. Talk with your grandchildren about the importance of having a common love for God with their future mates. Teach them the blessings received when God is the center of the marital relationship.

O Lord, match my grandchildren
with mates who love you with all their heart,
soul, mind, and strength. Amen.

Rejoice in Your Wife

May you rejoice in
the wife of your youth.

PROVERBS 5:18

Hollywood marriages seldom last.
Be thankful for your ordinary life.
Rejoice in the women your sons married
and thank God for your own husband.

❦

Jesus my Savior, thank you for
my husband and for the women my
sons married. May we all rejoice in the love
we've found in our mates. Amen.

Strive for God

For to this end we toil and strive,
because we have our hope set on the
living God, who is the Savior of
all men, especially of those who believe.

1 TIMOTHY 4:10 RSV

Children left to find God on their own usually don't. If your grandchildren have no Christian direction, you must toil and strive for them to know Christ as their Savior. Develop your relationship with them through e-mails, telephone calls, and time together so that the relationship grows into a mutual love for each other and for the Lord.

❧

Living God, urge my children to strive
to bring their children and others to
the knowledge of eternal
life through faith in you. Amen.

Hold Unswervingly
to Faith

*Let us hold unswervingly to the hope we
profess, for he who promised is faithful.*

HEBREWS 10:23

In a world of constant change, the Bible is
the firm, unshakable foundation of our
faith. Study the Bible so you know what
you believe and why. Instruct your
grandchildren to hold unswervingly to Jesus
Christ when worldly values conflict with
biblical truths.

*Jesus, strengthen my children, their mates,
and my grandchildren to hold unswervingly
to the hope they profess, for you
are faithful to your promises.
Amen.*

Memorize God's Word

*Fix these words of mine
in your hearts and minds.*

DEUTERONOMY 11:18

Memorization comes easy to a child. Teach your grandchildren Bible verses so God's Word will be fixed in their hearts and minds. You might even learn a few new verses along the way.

❦

Eternal God, fix your Word in the hearts and minds of my grandchildren. Amen.

Tithe

"Bring the whole tithe.... Test me in this," says the Lord Almighty, "and see if I will not throw open the floodgates of heaven and pour out so much blessing that you will not have room enough for it."

<small>MALACHI 3:10</small>

Tithing is the one thing that God says to test him on. Try it. Give to God first and see how he blesses you.

※

Lord Almighty, challenge my children and grandchildren to test you on the blessings they will receive when they tithe. Throw open the floodgates of heaven when they honor you with their firstfruits. Amen.

Mentor

Then [the older women] can train the younger women to love their husbands and children, to be self-controlled and pure, to be busy at home, to be kind, and to be subject to their husbands, so that no one will malign the word of God.

TITUS 2:4-5

Each generation learns from the previous one. What are your daughters learning from you? Mentor your daughters by your example on how to be loving, self-controlled, pure, hardworking, kind, and respectful.

Gracious God, help me to train my daughters to love their husbands and children as well as to be self-controlled, pure, busy at home, kind, and subject to their husbands. Amen.

Spiritual Leader

Fathers...bring [your children] up
in the training and instruction of the Lord.

EPHESIANS 6:4

Children look to their father for
spiritual leadership. Encourage your
sons to take the role of spiritual leader by
heading up family devotions, leading in
prayer, loving God's Word, and worshiping
regularly. Help them understand the
example they are setting for their sons.

Father God, guide my sons to lead
their families spiritually. Guide them to
bring their children up in the training and
instruction of the Lord. Amen.

Rest

There remains, then, a Sabbath-rest for the people of God; for anyone who enters God's rest also rests from his own work, just as God did from his.

HEBREWS 4:9-10

In our go-go society, we often feel guilty for resting. God designed rest. It is important that you rest from your work to be refreshed and to bring your focus back to God.

God, grant my husband a day of rest from his work and household chores so he may worship you unencumbered from his daily responsibilities. Amen.

Godly Friends

*Blessed is the man who does not
walk in the counsel of the wicked or
stand in the way of sinners or sit
in the seat of mockers.*

PSALM 1:1

Who are your friends? Are you listening to the advice of unbelievers or spending time with those who scoff at God? If so, experience the blessing of godly friends by getting to know people at church, Bible studies, and Christian fellowship events.

*Lord God, protect my dear ones
from walking in the counsel of the wicked
or standing in the way of sinners or
sitting in the seat of mockers. Bring godly
friends into their lives. Amen.*

Hear and Listen

Hear the word of the Lord. . . .
Listen to the teaching of our God.

ISAIAH 1:10 NRSV

Sometimes we fail to hear what others say because we are distracted by the TV, computer, or newspaper. Don't let your surroundings distract you from hearing the Word of the Lord and listening to his teachings. Make time to read the Bible, seek God in prayer, and listen for God's call.

Father God, open my husband's ears
to hear your Word and to
listen to your teaching. Amen.

Desire Spiritual Gifts

And in any event,
you should desire the most helpful gifts.

1 Corinthians 12:31 nlt

Young adults and college students often
flounder trying to figure out what to do
with their lives. Talk to your grandchildren
about the unique gifts you see in them.
Encourage them to use their talents in
service to God.

Loving Father, help my young adult
grandchildren to recognize
the spiritual gifts you have given them
and encourage them to use
their gifts in ministry for you. Amen.

Yearn for God

*My soul yearns, even faints,
for the courts of the Lord; my heart and
my flesh cry out for the living God.*

PSALM 84:2

As a grandmother, your heart yearns for
the next time you get to see your
children and hold your grandbabies. So too
are we to yearn for God. Desire to spend
time with God in worship, prayer, and
Bible study, and long for the day you will
meet your Savior.

*Living God, inspire my loved ones' souls
to yearn for you and stir
their hearts to cry out
to you. Amen.*

Dependent on God

When you bow down before the Lord
and admit your dependence on him,
he will lift you up and give you honor.

JAMES 4:10 NLT

Y ou become your own little god when
you depend on your abilities and
resources. Do not bow down to the false
god of self. Turn to the Lord, the only true
living God, and recognize your dependence
on him as Lord of your life.

Living Lord, I admit I am wholly
dependent on you. Enlighten my family
to understand their dependence on you as
well so you may lift them up and
give them honor. Amen.

Victorious

But thanks be to God, who
always leads us in victory through Christ.

2 CORINTHIANS 2:14 NCV

We cannot control the outcome of
sickness, sorrow, suffering, and the
unsaved. Turn these things over to Jesus.
Focus on his victory over sin, death, and the
devil and give thanks.

Holy God, thanks be to you
for leading my children, their spouses,
and our grandchildren in victory over sin
and worldly temptations. Amen.

Clear Conscience

Keep your conscience clear, so that,
when you are maligned,
those who abuse you for your good
conduct in Christ may be put to shame.

1 PETER 3:16 NRSV

Honor Christ by making godly life choices. Keep your conscience clear, knowing you have upheld biblical principles. Let those who ridicule or disparage you see God in action and be put to shame for their sins.

Holy Lord, keep my dear ones' consciences
clear so when they are maligned,
those who abuse them
may be put to shame. Amen.

Endure

*By your endurance
you will gain your souls.*

LUKE 21:19 NRSV

E ndurance is necessary in many areas of life. You need it to remain in a difficult marriage, to raise faith-filled children, to baby-sit young grandchildren, and to avoid conforming to a secular worldview. Endure to the end of this life, clinging to Christ, and you will gain your soul.

Jesus, grant to my children and grandchildren endurance to resist worldly temptations and thereby gain the salvation of their souls.
Amen.

Life

*God has given us eternal life, and this
life is in his Son. He who has
the Son has life; he who does not
have the Son of God does not have life.*

1 JOHN 5:11-12

Praise God that through faith in Christ
we have eternal life. Death is not the
end, but a new beginning of life forever
with Jesus. If you or your husband fears
aging and death, be assured that he who
has Jesus already has eternal life.

*Eternal God, assure my husband and
me that life is forever in you.
Lead us to totally trust in you. Amen.*

Accept Others

*Christ accepted you so you
should accept each other,
which will bring glory to God.*

ROMANS 15:7 NCV

Accept your children's spouses as part of
your growing family. If this is difficult
to do, look to Christ as your example. Build
up your children's marriages by lavishly
loving and freely forgiving.

*Jesus, help my husband and me to accept
and love our children's lifetime mates
as you have accepted and loved us.
Amen.*

Hospitable

Offer hospitality to one another
without grumbling.

1 PETER 4:9

Hospitality is a means to be a witness of God in your life. Don't focus on the physical appearance of your home, but rather the Holy Spirit's calling within you. Let your love for God be evident to all who enter your door.

Jesus, inspire my children and
grandchildren to offer hospitality to all
people, welcoming them in your name
and reflecting your love in their lives. Amen.

Confess Sins

I said, "I will confess my sins
to the Lord," and you forgave my guilt.

PSALM 32:5 NCV

Restoring a broken relationship is impossible without confessing your offense to the one you have offended. The same is true for your relationship with God. Come to God with a grieving heart for your disobedience and he will forgive you and remember your sins no more.

Lord, thank you that you forgive
my children and their spouses when they
confess their sins to you. Amen.

Zealous

*Never be lacking in zeal, but keep
your spiritual fervor, serving the Lord.*

ROMANS 12:11

Problems can get so overwhelming that
we lose our zeal, our spiritual fervor, and
our desire to serve the Lord. How do we
combat this? By focusing on the enormity
of God and not the size of the problem.

*Most Holy God, keep my family zealously
serving you, knowing that you are
bigger than any earthly problem. Amen.*

Act Justly

And what does the Lord require of you?
To act justly and to love mercy
and to walk humbly with your God.

MICAH 6:8

When your teenage grandchildren question what is expected of them, respond with God's answer: Be fair, forgiving, and faithful. Then show them how it is done. Deal honestly with friends and strangers alike, forgive generously, and follow God obediently each day.

Perfect God, help my teenage grandchildren to act justly, love mercy, and walk humbly with you. Amen.

Live by the Spirit

So I say, live by the Spirit,
and you will not gratify the desires
of the sinful nature.

GALATIANS 5:16

Through your own effort you cannot
resist worldly temptations. Give your life
to Christ and be led by the Spirit. When you
let God control your life, you will no longer
gratify the desires of your sinful nature.

Mighty Lord, spur my grandchildren
to live by the Spirit so they will not gratify
the desires of their sinful nature. Amen.

Child of God

We know that we are children of God and that all the rest of the world around us is under Satan's power and control.

1 JOHN 5:19 TLB

World leaders and other important people receive twenty-four-hour protection. You are an important person as a child of God and have been given eternal protection from hell. Evil can rage all around you, but God's security plan is impenetrable.

Heavenly Father, protect my family, your children, from the evils of this world. Amen.

Fear God

Blessed are all who fear the Lord,
who walk in his ways.... Your wife will
be like a fruitful vine within
your house; your sons will be like
olive shoots around your table.

PSALM 128:1, 3

How blessed you are if you have a family that loves the Lord and seeks to be obedient to his ways. Thank God today for the believers in your family. Pray every day for those who have not yet accepted Christ as their Savior.

Almighty God, I thank you for my children
and grandchildren who love you.
Bring into the family of faith those
who have not repented
and put their trust in you. Amen.

No Idols

*Those who cling to worthless idols
forfeit the grace that could be theirs.*

JONAH 2:8

P ower, money, success, and even our
children can become idols. What you
think about most, where you focus your
attention, or what you depend on when in
trouble, is your god. If you cling to anything
other than God, you are forfeiting the grace
that could be yours.

*Holy God, help my family to keep
from clinging to worthless idols and forfeiting
the grace that could be theirs. Amen.*

Persistent in Prayer

*And will not God bring about
justice for his chosen ones, who cry out
to him day and night?*

LUKE 18:7

A re you concerned for a loved one?
Are you on your knees day and
night asking God to hear your prayer?
How persistent are you?

*Merciful God, bring me to my knees
night and day seeking your face
for my family. Amen.*

Witnesses

*But you will receive power when the
Holy Spirit comes on you; and you will
be my witnesses...to the ends of the earth.*

ACTS 1:8

You have a powerful opportunity to be a
witness for Jesus with your grandchildren.
When the grandkids visit, make up songs
for Bible verses, draw prayer requests and
pray about them, or play charades with
favorite Bible stories. Boldly bring the
message of God's love and salvation to
those precious children in your care.

*Father, fill my grandchildren with your
Holy Spirit so they too may be
bold witnesses for you
all the days of their lives. Amen.*

Eyes on the Lord

We do not know what to do,
but our eyes are upon you.

2 CHRONICLES 20:12

Sometimes we just don't know what to do. Some of life's many choices include what job to take, which school to attend, and where to live. When your family asks for your advice, counsel them to spend time in prayer seeking God's will before they make a decision.

Ever-present God, lead my children
to look to you when they
do not know what to do. Amen.

Spotless

Make every effort to be found spotless,
blameless and at peace with [God].

2 PETER 3:14

The fingerprint-free stainless steel refrigerator allows you to touch it without leaving a mark. That is how we are to be. If sin and temptation touch us, we are to be found resistant and remain spotless.

❦

Holy God, lead my family to make
every effort to be found spotless, blameless,
and at peace with you. Amen.

Orderly

For God is not a God of disorder....
But everything should be
done in a fitting and orderly way.

1 CORINTHIANS 14:33,40

God's creation is orderly. The planets rotate around the sun, the earth makes a full turn every twenty-four hours, and the body's circulatory system distributes the perfect amount of blood and oxygen. Disorder brings discord that is never of the Lord, so establish orderliness in your household.

Creator God, guide my children
and their families to do everything in a
fitting and orderly way. Amen.

Encourage Self-Control

Encourage the young men
to be self-controlled.

In this age of instant gratification, self-control is hard. It takes self-control to turn off the video game to do schoolwork, walk away from the sexually explicit movie, and not flirt with the beautiful co-worker. Encourage the young men in your family to be self-controlled in all areas of their lives.

Holy God, guard the hearts of the
young men in my family.
Keep them steadfast in their walk
with you by encouraging one another
to exercise self-control. Amen.

Reconciled

*But now he has reconciled you by
Christ's physical body through death to
present you holy in his sight,
without blemish and free from accusation.*

COLOSSIANS 1:22

Family bickering and marital strife grieve
God and bring heartache to the family.
God provides healing and reconciliation
through Jesus Christ. Allow Jesus to permeate
your lives and see the healing begin.

*Heavenly Father, thank you for reconciling
our broken lives with you and with one
another, through Jesus. Protect my
children's marriages and family
relationships from Satan's efforts
to tear them down. Amen.*

Provided in Abundance

And God is able to provide you with
every blessing in abundance,
so that by always having enough of
everything, you may share
abundantly in every good work.

2 Corinthians 9:8 nrsv

God has abundantly blessed you with family. Your immediate family has expanded to include additional sons and daughters and grandchildren, so your love has grown and stretched to include everyone. Share that love abundantly.

Thank you, God, for providing me
with a growing family. You have blessed
us with abundance. Help us to share
abundantly in every good work. Amen.

Obedient

This is love for God;
to obey his commands.

1 JOHN 5:3

To obey God's commands you must know them. God's Word provides everything you need to know about God. As you daily read your Bible, ask the Holy Spirit to teach you God's will and how it applies to your life so you may be obedient.

Gracious God, may my precious family show their love for you by obeying your commands. Amen.

Rich in Good Deeds

*Command them to do good,
to be rich in good deeds, and to be
generous and willing to share.*

1 Timothy 6:18

You may not be rich in money, but you can be rich in good deeds. Be generous and willing to share your time and talents. Give your children a break from parenting and offer to take the grandkids to the local park or for the night.

*O Lord, direct my loved ones to do good,
to be rich in good deeds, and to be generous
and willing to share. Amen.*

Glad

I was glad when they said to me,
"Let us go to the house of the Lord!"

PSALM 122:1 NRSV

Being included makes people happy.
Welcome an unbeliever to your church.
Tell her about Jesus so she may be glad for
the invitation to come and worship in the
house of the Lord.

Jesus, embolden me to invite my
unbelieving family members to church
so together we may rejoice and be glad to
go to the house of the Lord. Amen.

Love Your Enemies

Listen, all of you. Love your enemies.
Do good to those who hate you.

LUKE 6:27 TLB

I t is so essential to love. Unloving Christians dishonor God, for God is love. Let your love for those who hate you be a powerful testimony of God's love for everyone.

Loving God, give to my children and
grandchildren a heart like yours that they
may love their enemies and do good to those
who hate them. Amen.

No Room for the Devil

And do not make room for the devil.

I f God fills your life, there is no room for
the devil. Seek the Holy Spirit's presence
each day, allowing the Word of God to
dwell in you richly, and let your mouth be
filled with praise. Hang out the "No Vacancy"
sign for Satan.

*Mighty Lord, protect my children and their
families from giving the devil any
opportunity to take up residency. Amen.*

Believe

*Believe on the Lord Jesus, and you will
be saved, you and your household.*

ACTS 16:31 NRSV

Even the devil knows Jesus. Don't just
know about Jesus, but believe in him
by trusting in him and putting him first in
your life. Worship, pray, learn from the
Bible, and be obedient to God so you may
lead your family by example to a personal
relationship with the risen Lord.

*Lead my household to believe in you,
Lord Jesus, through your Word
and my example. Amen.*

Pure

For God wants you to be holy and pure
and to keep clear of all sexual sin
so that each of you will
marry in holiness and honor.

1 Thessalonians 4:3-4 TLB

With society's portrayal of sex, purity before and during marriage seems pointless. However, the point is that God requires it. Sexual temptation is everywhere and a conscious attempt is required to avoid its trap.

Righteous God, keep my family holy
and pure. Guard each one from sexual sin
so that each may enter and honor their
marriage in purity. Amen.

Build Up Others

*Therefore encourage one another
and build up each other.*

1 THESSALONIANS 5:11 NRSV

We are called to build up each other
in the Lord. Strengthen your family's
faith by cheering them on in their prayer
life, encouraging them to know the Scriptures,
and supporting their fellowship with other
Christians. Actively take part in fortifying
their faith.

*Heavenly Father, prompt my children
and grandchildren to encourage one
another and build up
each other in the faith. Amen.*

Clean Heart

Create in me a clean heart,
O God. Renew a right spirit within me.

PSALM 51:10 NLT

During a visit from the grandkids, no matter how hard you work, you cannot keep up with the clutter. Similarly, no matter how hard you try, you cannot clean up your sin. Only Christ can create a clean heart and renew a right spirit within you.

❧

Create in my grandchildren a clean heart,
O God, and renew a right
spirit within them.
Amen.

Happiness

Happy are those who fear the Lord, who greatly delight in his commandments.

PSALM 112:1 NRSV

In the whole scheme of life, what you really want for your children is happiness. True happiness, however, doesn't come with success, vacations, or friends, but with a reverent fear of the Lord. Happiness is spending time with God and desiring to obey only him.

❧

Lord, teach my children and grandchildren to fear you with reverent awe and to delight in your Word. Amen.

Honor Parents

Honor your father and your mother,
so that your days may be long
in the land that the
Lord your God is giving you.

EXODUS 20:12 NRSV

Kids sometimes listen better to someone
other than their parents. Be that
someone. Teach your grandchildren the
respect and honor God requires of them
toward their parents.

❧

Faithful Lord, give my grandchildren
a desire to honor you by
honoring their parents.
Amen.

Faithful to Your Wife

So guard yourself in your spirit,
and do not break faith
with the wife of your youth.

<small>MALACHI 2:15</small>

No one enters marriage with plans of
unfaithfulness. You must actively
guard your heart, body, and mind from
anyone but your husband. Teach your sons
and grandsons to turn and run when
temptations come knocking.

❧

Jesus, thank you for my son's wife.
Protect my son and grandsons
from temptation and
keep their marriages strong. Amen.

Assured Understanding

I want their hearts to be encouraged and united in love, so that they may have all the riches of assured understanding and have the knowledge of God's mystery, that is Christ himself, in whom are hidden all the treasures of wisdom and knowledge.

Colossians 2:2-3 nrsv

This world doesn't provide much assurance. National security, personal safety, and financial stability are uncertain. Nevertheless, you can be fully assured that your eternity is secure in Jesus, who gives to you eternal life the moment you accept him as your Savior.

Father, give to my children and grandchildren understanding and knowledge of Jesus Christ. Amen.

Cling to the Lord

My soul clings to you;
your right hand upholds me.

PSALM 63:8 NRSV

Just as a drowning person clings to a life
preserver, you are to cling to God for
your salvation. Let go of the things that
pull you under, including sexually charged
TV shows and all ungodly behavior.

❧

Jesus, I pray that my family
will cling to you and that your right hand
will uphold them. Amen.

Sanctified

*May God himself, the God
of peace, sanctify you through and through.*

1 THESSALONIANS 5:23

God himself has set you apart from the world to be devoted to him. Through and through—body, mind, and spirit—you are different from the unbelieving world. Show that you are.

*God, sanctify my children and
grandchildren through and through for
your sacred purposes. Amen.*

Knowledgeable

*The fear of the Lord is
the beginning of knowledge.*

PROVERBS 1:7

Remember when you fell in love? You
spent every possible moment together
getting to know each other more fully.
Have you fallen in love with God? Do you
spend time getting to know him?

*All-knowing God, thank you for my
husband and for the love and memories
we share. Guide us to gain
a reverent fear of you by spending time
in your Word and in prayer. Amen.*

Just

*The Lord is just in all his ways,
and kind in all his doings.*

PSALM 145:17 NRSV

Parents frequently struggle to be just and fair with their children. God is just in all his ways and kind in all his doings. Let us pray to be more like him.

*Righteous God, make us more
like you by helping us to be just and
kind in all we do. Amen.*

See His Glory

The heavens are telling the glory of God; and the firmament proclaims his handiwork.

PSALM 19:1 NRSV

How magnificent is God's creation! Each twinkling star extols the glory of God. Each smiling face of a grandchild proclaims his handiwork.

Creator God, thank you for my grandchildren. Allow them to see the glory of your creation and give you thanks. Amen.

Hunger and Thirst
for Righteousness

*Blessed are those who hunger and thirst
for righteousness, for they will be filled.*

MATTHEW 5:6

Family mealtimes provide some of the best memories. Food and family laughter bring smiles all around. Fill your family with memories of how God has worked in your life and create a hunger and thirst for righteousness that only comes to those who desire to turn their life over to Christ.

*God, give to my family a true hunger
for your Word and let them be filled. Amen.*

Persevere

*Let us run with perseverance
the race marked out for us. Let us fix
our eyes on Jesus, the author and
perfecter of our faith.*

HEBREWS 12:1-2

Don't lose sight of the goal of eternity with God. Spiritual perseverance requires setting your sights on Jesus and training yourself in God's character. Jesus won your salvation, now finish the race with him.

*Jesus, encourage my extended and
blended family to run with perseverance
the race marked out for them,
fixing their eyes on you, the author and
perfecter of their
faith. Amen.*

Not Greedy

*Beware! Don't be greedy for what
you don't have. Real life is
not measured by how much we own.*

LUKE 12:15 NLT

The desire for more fascinates and then
assassinates. Greed feeds selfishness that
destroys dependence on God. Help the
breadwinners in your children's families to
know that no material possession can compare
to a vibrant and personal relationship with
Jesus Christ.

*Provider God, guard my children
and their families from wishing for what
they don't have, and teach them
that real life is not valued
by their earthly possessions. Amen.*

Trained in Godliness

Train yourself in godliness.

1 TIMOTHY 4:7 NRSV

Don't stagnate in the faith. Get active in training yourself in godliness by seeking out opportunities to learn more about God. Diligently examine God's Word, read Christian literature, listen to Christian speakers, attend Christian seminars, and share what you are learning with your family.

Dear Jesus, encourage my family to train themselves in godliness by actively seeking out Christian opportunities to learn more about you. Amen.

Wait Expectantly

I wait for the Lord, my soul waits,
and in his word I put my hope.

PSALM 130:5

We wait in checkout lines and in doctors' offices; we wait for news from the kids and answers from God. Sometimes we wait in irritation, anxiety, and impatience. As you expectantly wait for God's answers, rest assured that both his timing and his answers are perfect.

Sovereign Lord, as my family waits
expectantly for your answers to prayer, help
them to put their hope in you. Amen.

Share Faith

*I pray that you may be active
in sharing your faith, so that you will
have a full understanding of every
good thing we have in Christ.*

PHILEMON 1:6

Sharing the Christian faith is hard for a
lot of people. If that is true for you,
start with an easy audience. Talk to your
young grandchildren about God and why
he is important in your life; help them
express to you and others their love for God.

*Christ Jesus, motivate me to share
my faith and to teach my grandchildren to
actively share their faith as well
so they may have a full understanding of
every good thing we have in you. Amen.*

Heart and Soul for God

Love the Lord your God
with all your heart, all your soul, all
your strength, and all your mind.

LUKE 10:27 NCV

Love the Lord your God with your whole being. Love him emotionally, spiritually, bodily, and intellectually. Totally give your life to Christ.

Mighty Lord, I pray that my family
will love you with all their
heart, soul, strength, and mind. Amen.

Sufficient Grace

My grace is sufficient for you,
for my power is made perfect in weakness.

2 Corinthians 12:9

Y ou cannot control every life situation.
Be an example of a life dependent on
God. Let those around you see that in your
weakness God's power is made perfect and
his provision is sufficient.

In difficult times, dear Lord,
help my family learn that whatever you
provide for that moment is sufficient
if they put their trust in you.
Teach them that your power is made perfect
in their weakness. Amen.

Do Good

*May you always be doing those good,
kind things that show you are
a child of God, for this will bring much
praise and glory to the Lord.*

PHILIPPIANS 1:11 TLB

Look for positive behavior in your
grandchildren and compliment them.
Encourage future kindness by taking notice
today and giving praise. Let them know
that good, kind things show that they are
children of God and bring him glory.

*Holy Father, prompt my grandchildren
always to be doing those good, kind things
that show they
are your
children.
Amen.*

Do Not Misuse God's Name

*You shall not misuse the name of
the Lord your God, for the
Lord will not hold anyone guiltless
who misuses his name.*

Deuteronomy 5:11

Too often people exclaim surprise,
frustration, or fear by using God's name
without any thought of actually calling on
Almighty God. Teach your grandchildren
to use God's name only when praising him,
praying to him, or talking about him.

*Lord God, forgive us for misusing
your name. Guide my grandchildren to
honor you by reserving your name
for times of prayer and praise. Amen.*

Not Crushed by Trials

We are hard pressed on every side,
but not crushed; perplexed,
but not in despair.

2 CORINTHIANS 4:8

Problems sometimes bring on more problems. If your family is being pressed on every side, ask God for his strength to endure the trials. Trust God to keep you from despair and from being crushed.

Almighty God, preserve my family
from the trials pressing in on every side.
Fortify our faith so we are not
crushed or fall into despair. Amen.

Perspective From Suffering

*I consider that our present sufferings
are not worth comparing with the glory
that will be revealed in us.*

ROMANS 8:18

The physical, financial, or family
suffering we are currently enduring is
nothing when compared to spending an
eternity with God. Our attitude changes
when our perspective changes. Look at this
moment of suffering through God's lens of
eternity and take heart.

*Loving God, remind my family that the
present sufferings are not worth comparing
with the glory that is to come. Amen.*

Available

*Then I heard the voice of the Lord
saying, "Whom shall I send?
And who will go for us?" And I said,
"Here am I. Send me!"*

ISAIAH 6:8

You don't have to be a far-off missionary
to answer God's call. The hungry, poor,
lonely, and unsaved are closer than you
think. Be listening and available for God's
call to serve others in your community so
you can say, "Here I am. Send me."

*Living God, I pray that my loved ones
will be available when you call.
Help them to hear your voice and respond
with "Send me." Amen.*

Discerning Heart

So give your servant a discerning heart
to govern your people and
to distinguish between right and wrong.

1 Kings 3:9

A discerning heart is one that is perceptive to godly choices. Discernment is required to raise a godly family. Guide your family to pray for God's wisdom and discernment when making life choices.

All-knowing God, give my children
and their spouses discerning hearts so they
will raise their children to distinguish
between right and wrong. Amen.

Not Anxious

*Do not be anxious about anything,
but in everything, by prayer
and petition, with thanksgiving,
present your requests to God.*

PHILIPPIANS 4:6

id not God set the planets in motion
and put the sun in its place? Did not
your heavenly Father raise his only begotten
Son from the dead and honor him at his
right side? What is it that you are so anxious
about that is too big for God to handle?

*Almighty ever-living God, relieve my
family from anxiety
as they bring their
concerns to you.
Amen.*

Bearing Fruit

*[The righteous] will still bear fruit
in old age, they will stay fresh
and green, proclaiming, "The Lord
is upright; he is my Rock,
and there is no wickedness in him."*

PSALM 92:14-15

Keep going. Don't stop working for the
Lord, thinking you've taken your turn
and it is time to let someone else do it.
Encourage your husband to join you in
bearing fruit for the Lord by volunteering,
taking a mission trip, or driving an elderly
person to church.

*Holy God, keep my husband and me
bearing fruit for you, knowing
that you are our Rock and will support us
in all we do for you. Amen.*

Receive Salvation

You have been taught the holy Scriptures
from childhood, and they
have given you the wisdom to receive
the salvation that comes
by trusting in Christ Jesus.

2 TIMOTHY 3:15 NLT

D o your grandchildren know the Holy
Scriptures? Encourage them to get to
know Jesus by giving them their own Bible.
Read the Bible together so that they will
know God's plan of salvation.

❧

Christ Jesus, guide my grandchildren
to know the Holy Scriptures and
have the wisdom to receive
your salvation through faith. Amen.

Faithfulness

Be faithful until death,
and I will give you the crown of life.

REVELATION 2:10 NRSV

God doesn't judge you on results, but on faithfulness. In obedience to God's calling and his will, keep sharing the good news of Jesus Christ with your family. The outcome of your efforts is in God's hands—whether you are faithful, is in yours.

❦

Christ Jesus, keep my family faithful
until death so they may
receive the crown of life. Amen.

Pray for Life

I love the Lord because he hears my
prayers and answers them.
Because he bends down and listens,
I will pray as long as I have breath!

PSALM 116:1-2 TLB

As a Christian grandmother you have spent many hours in prayer for your family. God has heard your prayers during sleepless nights and joy-filled days. May your legacy be that you continued to pray even with your last breath.

Heavenly Father, thank you for
hearing and answering my
prayers. Help my
family to recognize the
privilege of praying as long as
they have breath. Amen.

Overflow With Love

My prayer for you is that you will
overflow more and more with
love for others, and at
the same time keep on growing
in spiritual knowledge and insight.

<small>PHILIPPIANS 1:9 TLB</small>

M ake this verse your grandmotherly
prayer. Seek God's face for your
family that they will overflow more and
more with love for one another and that
they will keep growing in spiritual knowledge
and insight. Pray persistently to this end.

❧

Dear God, I pray that my whole family
will overflow with love for one another and
at the same time keep on growing in
spiritual knowledge and insight. Amen.

About the Author

NANCY ANN YAEGER is a mother of three, wife, homemaker, attorney, and author of *A Mother's Prayers for Her Children*. She is the Minnesota Prayer Coordinator for Moms In Touch International (MITI) and publishes a weekly prayer newsletter for the Minnesota leaders and members of MITI. Nancy Ann spends her free time on the sidelines cheering on her children playing sports. She enjoys jet skiing, and watching movies with her husband in their home in Minnesota.

Acknowledgments

Thank you to the grandmothers I consulted to gain insights for this book. I want to especially thank my own mother, Nancy Engle, who faithfully prays for her children and grandchildren and who is a steadfast example of how to live for God. I would also like to thank Dorothy Larson and Diane Miller, who are fervent praying grandmothers and who shared their personal desires and prayers for their families to help me gain a better understanding of a grandmother's heart. Finally heartfelt thanks goes to: Kyle, Julie, and their colleagues at Bethany House who excel at making the author look good; my Moms In Touch sisters, especially Jewel and Deanna, who kept me in their prayers; my dad, Don Engle, who is my biggest fan; my husband, Greg, and my children, Dan, Allison, and Paul, who cheer me on and have seen God's hand in the whole publishing process.

Godly Character and Virtues Index

295

Scripture Index